Dr Denis Biggart was born in 1936 in Edinburgh. In 1937 he moved to Belfast when his father became Professor of Pathology at Queen's University. He received a broad education in science and classics at the Royal Belfast Academical Institution, where he also played rugby for the 1st XV. In 1961 he qualified in medicine at Queen's and opted to follow a postgraduate career in pathology gaining an M.D. (Hons.) in 1965. He won a Fulbright Scholarship to Johns Hopkins Hospital, Baltimore, 1967–8, gaining further valuable experience in diagnostic pathology and research. On return to Belfast he became Lecturer in the Institute of Pathology and was promoted to Senior Lecturer/Consultant in 1970. He moved to the Belfast City Hospital Laboratory in 1973 acting as Consultant Pathologist to the City Hospital, whilst continuing to lecture to undergraduates at the Royal Victoria Hospital. He became Head of the City Hospital Histopathology Department in 1992 and continued in this role until his retirement in 1997. Throughout his career he was a keen undergraduate and postgraduate teacher and involved in numerous Health Service, University and Postgraduate Educational committees. From 1981–91 he was Regional Adviser to the Royal College of Pathologists.

For all the Biggart family and John Henry's
students and close colleagues who
he considered part of his extended family.

JOHN HENRY BIGGART

Pathologist, Professor and Dean of Medical Faculty, Queen's University, Belfast

DENIS BIGGART

ULSTER HISTORICAL FOUNDATION

Front cover: John Henry Biggart on roof of Pennsylvania Hotel, New York in transit to Johns Hopkins Hospital, Baltimore, USA

First published 2012
by Ulster Historical Foundation
49 Malone Road, Belfast, BT9 6RY
www.ancestryireland.com
www.booksireland.org.uk

© Denis Biggart
ISBN: 978-1-908448-10-1

Printed by W&G Baird Ltd.
Design by Cheah Design

CONTENTS

LIST OF ILLUSTRATIONS

FOREWORD

John Henry Biggart was, quite simply, the most creative force in Ulster medicine in the twentieth century, perhaps ever. Through sheer ability, strength of personality, a clear and prophetic vision of how things should be (and in fact largely became), and the zeal and confidence to pursue it, he precociously gained and held for long, often very long, periods, key positions in Queen's University, the health services in Northern Ireland, the General Medical Council and many other important bodies. No-one before or since has wielded such power and influence in Ulster medicine, and he wielded them with an almost faultless touch during a lengthy period of unprecedented structural changes in the profession. To thousands of Queen's medical graduates he was an iconic figure; a gifted teacher, an effective administrator, an industrious if demanding senior, and ever a straight-dealer – you always knew where you were with him even if you didn't much like the place!

His achievements are widely acknowledged though, remarkably for such a towering figure, incompletely chronicled. For all his successes and extensive activities little is known of the man himself other than that gleaned from his public *persona*. His public lectures, speeches and pronouncements added little relevant beyond his classical learning and a disciple's regard for the physician-philosopher, Sir William Osler. He gave no interviews. Though companionable he was neither gregarious nor an enthusiastic host, so there were very few occasions when convivial exchanges might have disclosed something more beyond what was on view. His innermost thoughts, if divulged at all, were reserved for confidants. I worked closely and amicably with him when I was Dean of the Faculty of Medicine in the year before his retirement in 1971, but when I was honoured by his family in giving the panegyric at his funeral I could only add to his known attributes an unsuspected taste for classical music and a suspected one for the standard English literature canon, and confirm his unrivalled talent for delegating paper-work, which he loathed!

His son, Dr Denis Biggart, like his father a pathologist, an RBAI pupil, a Queen's graduate and who was also a consultant member in his father's Department, has in this intriguing, informative and entertaining book, now swept aside the veil. Drawing on his own extensive knowledge and experience of his father's work, at home and at play, and on unpublished autobiographical notes, philosophical ruminations, random musings and more organised sections including verse and reminiscences, which his father had jotted down from time to time 'for my own delectation and to place on record those episodes which bubble up through the morass of memory ... [and] for me alone, for my enjoyment, but if others care to read some name, some place, may evoke for them too, fond memory', he presents a John Henry Biggart rarely, imagined: a man of wide culture, of deep sensitivities – albeit of stern intellectual integrity, a man of wit and humour with a wide romantic streak and who enjoyed nothing better than an evening of quiet domesticity reading and re-reading the English classics, listening to classical music, smoking his pipe, and enjoying his quiet fireside with his wife, Isobel.

The author is never less than faithful to fact and enlivens his story with telling anecdotes and well-selected illustrations, mostly photographs now seen for the first time outside the family. Each chapter yields fresh insights into the personality and motivations of this unusually private man, a man who rarely voiced (as distinct from formed) his opinions of others, especially critical ones, and seems seldom if ever to have borne grudges or shown vindictiveness or spite. The reader is therefore not side-tracked from the thrust of the narrative and the important new biographical information by descriptions of unimportant personal rivalries and petty intrigues which so often distract rather than inform.

John Henry Biggart died on 21st May 1979, aged 73, while on his way to attend a GMC meeting in London. He would have welcomed such a death, sudden and while in harness, a playing out of his favourite quotation 'Cease not 'till day streams to the west; then down that estuary, drop down in peace'.

Everyone who knew, or knew of, Sir John Henry Biggart, who has profited from the medical education which he largely authored or the professional training programmes which he largely instigated and supervised, or who has wondered how the Queen's Medical School grew from provincial status to national importance often punching above its weight, should welcome and possess this book which now fills a yawning gap in the 176-year Belfast Medical School's historiography. On these and other counts I can heartily recommend it.

Sir Peter Froggatt
(Formerly Dean of the Faculty of Medicine and President and
Vice-Chancellor of the Queen's University Belfast)

PREFACE

My father, John Henry Biggart, was the eldest child of a country schoolmaster and schoolmistress from County Antrim. He excelled at school and university and was appointed Professor of Pathology at Queen's University, Belfast when aged thirty-one. Seven years later he was also elected Dean of the Faculty of Medicine and was annually re-elected for an unprecedented twenty-seven years. Generations of students revered him for his orderly, lucid and amusing lectures and, importantly, regarded him as a 'father figure' in whom they could repose complete trust and from whom they could expect wise counsel and fair play. His administrative abilities and increasing authority were not limited to Queen's and the Royal Victoria Hospital, the main teaching hospital beside which the Institute of Pathology was sited, but grew with the Province-wide introduction of the National Health Service and post-graduate medical education machinery so that, through the administrative and advisory committee structures and sheer force of personality and ability, my father came to exert a dominant influence over the entire medical scene in Northern Ireland. He also ably represented Queen's and the Province's medical interests, as well as contributing nationally, through long service (27 years) on the General Medical Council which ended only with his sudden death in harness on 21st May 1979 aged seventy-three.

Towards the end of his life my father turned to reminiscing. In the evening he would sit in his favourite armchair beside the inevitable coal fire, sip Black Bushmills whiskey and puff his pipe, and jot down his early memories to be put later in coherent form. Unfortunately death intervened before completion. However, my mother readily granted permission to release the unpublished material to Dr John Weaver who used it as a basis for his Presidential Address to the Ulster Medical Society in 1985* and this remains the only worthwhile biographical sketch and assessment of my father. These notes are now in my possession and I have tried to meld them into a more extensive story of his life. From my unique position as being his only son and moreover also a Queen's-trained pathologist I was able to observe him as a father and family man as well as a lecturer, professor, Dean, director of specialist training and research, and administrator. I hope that I may succeed in the following chapters to portray something of his considerable talents and the nature of his complex character, sometimes appearing as a reincarnation of a stern Victorian *paterfamilias* in the formality of his dress, domestic routine and adherence to strict ethical standards; sometimes presenting as an awe-inspiring gruff and severe figure to those who dared to obstruct his intentions or frustrate his ambitions; whilst at other times radiating geniality, charm and humour. Yet he was ever a dreamer at heart, something of a romantic if a seemingly unlikely one, and an innovative visionary of the course to be plotted for Northern Ireland medicine which would be effective, efficient, fair and up-to-date and at all times preserve the best tenets of the 'Art' – which he tracked back in a discontinuous line to the classical Greece of the medical schools of Cnidos and Cos, which was the subject of his valedictory address to the Ulster Medical Society on his retirement in 1971. He was a man whom my sister Rosemary and I are proud to call our father.

---

* Weaver J.A.: 'John Henry Biggart, 1905–1979: A portrait in respect and affection'. *Ulster Medical Journal*, 1985 vol. 54 (1); pp 1–19.

ACKNOWLEDGEMENTS

I owe a great debt of gratitude to Sir Peter Froggatt who urged me towards the finishing line, when my efforts were flagging. He also kindly offered to edit the text which he accomplished meticulously, making numerous helpful suggestions along the way and furthermore, did not hesitate to agree to write the Foreword.

Thanks are also due to the following:

Professor Richard Clarke who smoothed the path to publication.

Dr Barry Kelly, Editor of the *Ulster Medical Journal* who allowed me free access to the Archives.

Professor Peter Toner, Editor of *Pathology at the Royal, the First Hundred Years; 1890–1990*, for allowing me to use any relevant information from its contents.

The late Mr Bert Russell, M.L.S.O., who showed me his collection of relevant newspaper cuttings and photographs taken in the RVH Pathology Laboratory.

Mr Maurice Taggart, M.L.S.O., who provided me with a list of his early memories of working in the RVH Pathology Laboratory.

Professor Alan Crockard, F.R.C.S., who readily agreed to my using an extract from my father's funeral panegyric after the premature death of his first wife, Mo.

Mrs Aileen McClintock, Deputy Keeper of Records, and Mr David Huddleston, Head of Records, Public Record Office of Northern Ireland for arranging the release of minutes from the Cameron Commission's interviews.

The *Daily Mail* for granting me permission to include the cartoon by Emmwood (John Musgrave-Wood) published after the publication of the Cameron Report, 1969.

Mr and Mrs Ray Gibson and Mrs Arlene McFarlane for relating their memories of Ballygowan and Carrickmannon School and arranging for me to meet Mrs Dora Thompson (née Anderson), a contemporary schoolmate of my father.

Finally, my cousin, Mrs Gillian Morrison (née Stewart) who provided me with a photograph of Carrickmannon schoolchildren in 1916, published in the *Mourne Observer*.

Chapter 1

A country boy

'I was conceived in County Clare' – so wrote my father at the start of his reminiscences. Not many of us are so certain of the place of our conception, but this statement provides an insight into his character which may explain much of his success in life in getting things done. He had an inner confidence and assertiveness which persuaded him and usually, but not always, others, that he was right.

My grandparents were both national schoolteachers in Ireland and at that time my grandfather held the post of Principal of a school in Ennis, County Clare. The reason for his having migrated south to Clare is unknown; he was a North Antrim man and the Biggart family, originally from Ayrshire, Scotland, had shown a general tendency over several centuries to remain within the confines of that county. He had previously been Principal in the school at Stranocum, County Antrim and it was there that he fell for and eventually married one of his former pupils, Mary Gault, also from County Antrim stock. My grandmother opted to move to the 'big city' of Belfast for the momentous event, the birth of her son. She is said to have had no doubts that it would be a son, and she was right! She obviously was the one who transmitted the genes of assertiveness to my father. Thus, my father came into the world on 17th November 1905 at Stranmillis Road, Belfast, where my grandmother's sister lived. The accoucheur was Dr McKenzie of University Square, who weighed in the newcomer at 12lbs. High birth weight is often a sign of maternal diabetes or pre-diabetes, but my grandmother never developed diabetes in her 79 years of life. It seems more likely that the scales were in error or that Dr McKenzie had fortified his medical courage with a dram on the way to the delivery at Stranmillis Road. My grandmother was apparently concerned at the size of the baby's head, but Dr McKenzie gave her some reassurance by stating: 'With a head that size, he is either a hydrocephalic or the future Lord Chancellor'. I am sure that

Dr McKenzie was accustomed to making such flattering pronouncements about most of his successful deliveries, but from that day on my grandmother was convinced that nothing but fame and distinction lay ahead of her 'wee Harry'. The baby was duly christened John Henry – the same name as his father: so only the close family and his later Ballygowan friends called him Harry and he was eventually generally referred to as 'John Henry', especially amongst the medical profession.

After my father's birth the family decided to move north again and settled in the old Unitarian Manse near Templepatrick. My grandfather resumed teaching and kept my grandmother busy raising a family, for it was not long before my father gained two sisters – first Moira, then Florence. His brother, Hugh, who became an Ear, Nose and Throat surgeon, was an 'afterthought' and was twelve years his junior. Life in the country must have been very busy and there seems to have been little time to devote to babies. Certainly my father is said not to have uttered any recognisable mature words until well into his third year. He was to make up for this sluggish start later. Another indication of parental inattention occurred when his parents were visiting friends at a nearby farm. Whilst the adults were having afternoon tea, baby John Henry crawled unnoticed from the drawing room and across the kitchen, and into an adjacent outhouse where the milk was churned. The churn consisted of a large revolving vat set into the floor and filled to the brim with the herd's output for that day into which the baby proceeded to tumble headfirst. Fortunately, a farmhand heard his cries, fished him out with a stick and all was well. Psychiatrists now tell us that events which occur during babyhood significantly influence behaviour in adult life. I have, therefore, always wondered whether this near catastrophe had a profound effect on my father's future choice of beverages. Milk had a very low rating.

At the age of four he was already showing a streak of determination and self-will, traits that were to become so ingrained in later life. One day he donned his cap and coat and left home forever. He had got as far as the main Antrim Road before he was found and cajoled into returning and giving home another chance.

It is of interest that the so-called 'Unitarian manse' had previously been the home of the Reverend Robert Campbell, a minister in the Non-Subscribing Presbyterian Church, and his family. He was the father of John and Robert who were subsequently to make their mark in the development of medical services in Northern Ireland. John was Assistant Surgeon at the

Royal Belfast Hospital for Sick Children (1891–2), then in Queen Street, before becoming 'Assistant Physician' (in fact a gynaecologist) at the Samaritan Hospital, Lisburn Road. He remained on the staff for 30 years and played a crucial role in the hospital's development (as his son, William, was to do later) and received a knighthood. Robert was also Surgeon to the hospital in Queen Street from 1897 and then also on the consulting ('Visiting') staff of the Royal Victoria Hospital from 1900 until his early death in 1920. He was a quiet innovator of new ideas and techniques and is commemorated by the Ulster Medical Society in the annual Robert Campbell Oration, which my father was honoured to give in 1948 and was entitled 'The Contribution of Pathology to our Knowledge of the Internal Environment'.

The Campbell brothers were apparently taciturn men. The story is told that when, as undergraduates, they lived on University Road, they were disturbed at breakfast by the lowing of cattle. John got up, looked out, and said, 'Cows'; Robert followed him to the window and said, 'Bullocks'. A period of silence ensued. At the end of the meal, Robert suggested that they should live apart as there was 'too much argument in the house'. They parted soon after. Yet my father recalls that the Campbell boys in their younger days had had their lighter moments. At the rear of the Templepatrick manse there was a duck pond; it was here that the young Campbells were reputed to have sewn peas on a length of linen thread and fed them to the ducks. The poor creatures were only able to attain their freedom when each pea had been digested.

South Antrim was John Henry's home territory for his first seven years, but it was the northern part of the county which attracted his deepest affection. This seems to have been partly because his family ties lay there. On the Biggart side his ancestors had come to settle in North Antrim from Ayrshire, Scotland, in the early fifteen hundreds. (One of their offspring, Robert Biggart, was the first town-leet of Ballymoney in 1600, and was paid two pounds a year for ensuring that the curfew bell was rung each night). John Henry's mother's family were Gaults from Ballynure, near Larne. One, William Gault, was secretary of the South Antrim division of the United Irishmen in 1798. John Henry's maternal great-grandfather was killed on the hunting field and left a dozen children. These became scattered, his maternal grandfather settling in North Antrim and the Biggart-Gault consummation resulted. I remember accompanying my father in the latter years of his life on

John Henry's father (1915)

a journey to the old Parish church of Billy near Bushmills. He was convinced that we would discover the Biggart name engraved on some of the overgrown and lichen-covered headstones. Our diligent search proved to be in vain and we concluded that, as we were of Presbyterian stock, our ancestors had probably been buried in unmarked graves in unconsecrated ground outside the graveyard wall.

Throughout his life John Henry maintained this almost obsessional love for the rugged scenery of North Antrim with its cliffs and foaming seas, but most of all for its inhabitants. He reminded me of how it had been populated by a curious, but attractive, blend of the people of the Glens and of those Scots who had made their perilous voyage past Rathlin Island, past Fair Head to Murlough Bay or Ballycastle; or had wended their way through the rocky outcrops to Ballintoy. These were hard men who had conquered many difficulties and obstacles of nature. They had come, not to the broad rolling arable acres of subsequent Ulster planters, but to hostile rock and hill. They were tough, yet over the years they contributed to one of the most liberal communities in Ireland. The Glensmen also had had to eke out a living from the infertile soil. Scot and Glensman inhabited the same corner of the island and had a mutual respect for each other. One of my father's vivid memories was at his maternal grandfather's funeral. When he looked back from the top of the hill on the way to the cemetery he saw a cortege of marching men of all denominations stretching back for at least a mile. Such a memory has a special poignancy for us today as we survey the current political scene.

As regards my father's parents, both were of Presbyterian stock and held the strict puritanical views that were prevalent in those days. They attended church each Sunday morning and evening with their children who also had to go to Sunday school at 10.30am and 3pm. At Sunday school they had amongst other things to learn to recite the 119th Psalm (all 176 verses) and also the whole of the Shorter Catechism with proofs. Sunday was a day of absolute rest and no work of any sort was to be undertaken lest it incurred God's wrath. Both parents were teachers and I think good teachers who ruled by the cane if not with a rod of iron. I did not know my grandfather well, but he would occasionally visit our house when I was a young boy. He was also named John Henry and was ten years older than my grandmother. I remember him sitting in the armchair beside the fire reading the newspaper. He did not seem to indulge in much conversation and certainly had limited tolerance of his

Formal photograph of John Henry's mother (1916)

grandchildren: he probably had had a surfeit of children's behaviour during a lifetime of teaching and in raising his own family. He tended to intimidate my cousins and myself by suddenly quizzing us on our mathematical skills even though I was only seven when he died. I was fascinated by the halo of short grey curls which surrounded an austere face dominated by an aquiline nose. He was always dressed immaculately in a grey suit and a whiter-than-white shirt with stiffly starched collar and bow tie. It seemed in no way out of keeping that this man expected my grandmother to address him as 'Sir' in front of the schoolchildren. Nevertheless he was regarded as a superb teacher and was held in high respect by his pupils. I remember one tender moment when I was about five. We were alone in the garden when he suddenly crouched down and pulled out a small plant with an oval green leaf from the weed-strewn lawn. He told me that it was called sorrel and was good to eat. I still recall its acrid taste. From his own children he demanded the highest standards. Once when John Henry was in his early teens he returned home with his school report feeling quite pleased with his achievements having attained high marks in all subjects including 96% in mathematics. His father took a different viewpoint. 'Mathematics is an exact science. You ought to have scored 100%. Get upstairs to your desk and make sure you do better the next time.'

Carrickmannon School children with John Henry encircled in the back row (1916)

My grandmother was of a much more amiable disposition with a great sense of humour and she could readily dissolve into hearty laughter. She was a tall woman with broad shoulders and a plump chest. I remember her as having white hair, sometimes slightly crimped and singed from the use of hair tongs warmed in a coal fire. Her liberation in later life led to her occasionally sporting a blue rinse. She had a dominant personality – she had to have to stand up to my grandfather. Her main strengths lay in her pride in all her children and her ardent ambitions for them to succeed in life. She was also almost entirely responsible for holding the family circle together in her later years. She would pop into her Morris 8 and do the rounds of her children's families, transmitting the news good or bad. A very large leather bag with long handles always accompanied her from which she would sooner or later produce her knitting. Many a time she would ask me to hold out my arms to receive a skein of wool. Then, with flailing hands, she would rapidly roll the wool into a compact ball. Most of my school socks and sweaters were the results of her endeavours. Her only fault as far as I was concerned, was her very rough application of a facecloth and cold water when washing a child's face.

In 1912 my grandparents moved from their beloved County Antrim to County Down. My grandfather took up an appointment in Ballygowan

Carrickmannon School, Ballygowan, as it is today

National School before moving in 1914, now with his wife, to the small Carrickmannon School two miles outside the town on the Killyleagh Road, a mixed school formerly controlled by a brother and sister, both Roman Catholics. Following the appointment of the Biggarts the local priest pulled out all the pupils of his faith and established them in a neighbouring barn. Before this, in County Antrim, my father had never been aware of sectarian division in the community, though being only seven years old at the time might have been something to do with it. He had nevertheless recognised the diversity of religious denominations in that his family attended the Presbyterian Church whilst the family friends went to the Church of Ireland and the housekeeper to the Roman Catholic Chapel. It had seemed to him as a small boy that where you went on Sundays was simply dependent on the sort of family into which you had been born.

Carrickmannon School was at this time a quaint little building surmounted by a small bell-tower. It had two large classrooms of equal size in which children of differing ages and ability were taught. Their concentration was all the better focussed for the prominent display of a long flexible cane on the wall of each room and it was only on rare occasions that my grandparents had to apply it to the palms or rear end of an inattentive or mischievous child. According to one of my father's contemporaries (Dora

7

Anderson), John Henry was on one occasion hauled out in front of the class to become the recipient of such treatment seemingly in order to emphasise that he was not exempt by reason of being the son of the Principal. My grandfather, however, refused to discipline erring girl students who were passed to my grandmother for attention. The standards of education achieved seem to have been high and the school inspectors on their regular visits wrote glowing reports. Many years later, my grandmother was to run foul of the new beliefs in children's rights and the banishment of corporal punishment. She had officially retired but was acting as a locum teacher (1951–60) in Blaris School, Lisburn, when she found it necessary to cane a miscreant. The following day she was confronted on the school doorstep by the boy's parents who demanded to know what she meant by hitting their 'wee Willie'. She fortunately escaped without litigation.

The reputation of the little school grew steadily throughout the stewardship of the Biggarts. My grandfather remained Principal from 1914 until 1923 when he left to take up a more prestigious appointment at the Simpson Memorial School in East Belfast, where in 1926 he became Principal for the rest of his working life. On his departure my grandmother was immediately promoted to Principal of Carrickmannon, a post she retained until her retirement in 1950 even though it meant her travelling daily to Ballygowan from the new family home in Belfast. The appointment of my grandfather to the Belfast school resulted in the family vacating their Ballygowan residence in 1925 and moving to the city at 103, The Mount, just off Castlereagh Street. When the government of the day considered closing Carrickmannon in 1974 to save money by merging it with the large public school in nearby Ballygowan, the local population so vociferously opposed it that the Government relented, and to this day it continues its successful existence. On Friday, 27th November 1970, my father unveiled a wall plaque commemorating the association of the Biggart family with the school over a period of nearly sixty years. This took into account the fact that my Aunt Florence, my father's sister, also taught there as second teacher from 1951 until 1976.

It was at Carrickmannon Primary School that my father received his early educational grounding under the strict surveillance of his teacher parents. The family first set up residence in a house in Ravara, a townland close to the school, but within a few years moved to a large house overlooking the Square in Ballygowan. A mile and a half up the road lived the retired

Principal of Carrickmannon and when sectarian feelings ran high, amidst the atmosphere prevailing throughout Ireland in 1916, gossip had it that he thought that if he destroyed the Biggarts it would enhance the prospects for a united Ireland. So, once in a while, he would start down that mile and a half with a shotgun on his shoulder. Fortunately for the Biggarts his walk took him past 'Henry's of the Cross', a typical Irish public house at the crossroads. Here, gossip added, he would pause to fortify himself for the rest of the journey and the dreadful deed that lay ahead. After several pints of Guinness, however, the notion would wear off, at least until the next time. Actually, my father later found him to be quite a nice old man who occasionally chatted to him over his garden wall. Whether he ever accepted the Biggarts as part of the local community was a different matter.

Next door to the family residence lived the landlord, a pleasant, rather obese and well-to-do Roman Catholic. During the 'troubles' of that time he was said to be under some pressure from the local parish priest – a man considered by my father to have a great but not particularly saintly character – to remove the Biggarts from their rented house but he always refused to do so. One day my father spotted three parallel cuts on the landlord's bald head. On inquiry, he was told that the priest, wielding a brass candlestick from the altar, had inflicted the injuries as a disciplinary measure. It remained uncertain as to whether the 'disciplinary measure' was for his failure to evict the Biggarts or for some other misdemeanour.

Thus John Henry lived in the village of Ballygowan from the age of seven and through his teens. These are the formative years of development and the influences that he encountered at this time were all-important in setting the pattern for his later successes.

He attended Carrickmannon Primary School and was taught by his parents who demanded the highest standards and expected him to set an example to the other pupils. I rather think that he had extra parental tuition when required. Several years ago I met a member of my golf club who, on learning my identity, remembered my father being confined to his house, where he could be seen framed in the window, studying at his desk, whilst the other village lads were kicking a football on the road. Yet he was not regarded as a swot – he was an all-rounder and showed equal enthusiasm for sporting activities as soon as he had completed his studies. On one such occasion in his early teens, he turned out for the Ballygowan soccer team in the summer league. He was playing as centre-forward and had in some way offended an opposing player who proceeded to put his fists up and advance with intent on this relatively young schoolboy. With the irrational exuberance of youth John Henry stood his ground. Fortunately the Ballygowan fullback was the local blacksmith – a tall quiet man with rippling muscles developed at the anvil. John Henry felt himself being gently but firmly removed from the front line by the blacksmith who glowered and towered over the adversary. The smith made no aggressive move; he just stood and looked whilst the opposing player decided that discretion was the better part of valour and returned to his place on the field. After the match my father sought to thank him, but all he got was a growl: 'Youngsters should avoid getting involved in such things.'

Another great influence on his life was the Rev. Dr William Kerr McLernon, who was the minister of Ballygowan Presbyterian Church from 1900 till 1945. This educated gentleman took a profound interest in bright young Biggart and treated him as an adult even at the early age of seven. Occasionally he would call to take my father for lunch at the Slieve Donard Hotel, Newcastle. Afterwards they would sit in the sunshine and discuss, as if between equals, all the problems of the world. This association and friendship lasted through boyhood and into manhood, although apparently my grandmother was not quite as enamoured of 'His Reverence' and resented his tendency to meddle too much in the management of 'her' school. However, he also established a church lending library as a personal gift and so my father was introduced to the exciting adventure stories of G.A. Henty and revelled in Marshall Kent's exploits in Eastern Europe or the rides on the Scottish Borders or the wars in Wales. He then graduated to Conan Doyle and by the age of fifteen he had read much of Scott, Dickens and Thackeray. Thus was sown the seed that was to sprout into a lifelong love of reading which was later to bring him such solace, come riot, bomb, frayed tempers at committees, or frustration with work. Gradually he set aside the novels and replaced them by history, biography and literary essays. An hour of quiet reading always restored his equanimity. Towards the end of his life he was re-reading a volume of George Gissing's *Essays* when he discovered an inscription on its flyleaf, which he had written fifty years previously. It still remained as apt as ever – 'omnibus quietum quaesivi, sed nunquam inveni salve in angulo cum libro' – translating as 'in all things have I sought peace, but never have I found it save in a corner with a book.' He was a frequent browser in Mullen's bookstore in Donegall Place, Belfast and was one of its best customers, having an arrangement that the owners draw his attention to the best new issues.

While living in Ballygowan John Henry had the opportunity to visit several of the nearby 'gentlemen's residences', which made him aware of the graciousness of living enjoyed by some of the more wealthy members of the community. He saw the collections of beautiful antiques and bric-a-brac; he noted the supreme craftsmanship in the Chippendales, the Sheratons and the Heppelwaites, used then as ordinary chairs; he was overawed by the beauty of the china figures and the large gold-framed paintings that adorned the walls. Thus from an early age he held the ambition to live surrounded by objects of beauty, an aim partly frustrated by the punitive taxes of especially the nineteen-forties and fifties when he was actively collecting, but his eventual family home nevertheless was packed in Victorian fashion with artefacts and paintings, most of which he acquired at home auctions. These were his extravagances and savings. As long as he had enough money to live with these comforts around him he was content. He had otherwise very little interest in money and refused to devote time to dabbling in stocks and shares.

Yet it was the intimacy of village life that charmed him most of all. Presiding over the village, like a miniature Witenagemot, the supreme Anglo-Saxon Council, were the parson, the priest, the doctor and the squire. Each of these men exerted his influence over his flock, acting individually, but as if in concert, and so creating an atmosphere of entity and belonging. The country came through the village and pure undiluted country beauty surrounded it. Everyone that passed bade each other 'good morning'. Everyone knew everybody else and about their families and business. Even the names of their dogs, cows, horses and donkeys became familiar. All knew who had a notion of whom and that Mrs X had to spend periods of rest in the 'big house'. The word spread that Miss Y had finally admitted, after her third love child, that 'men were not to be trusted'. Miss Z, the daughter of a former minister, distributed 'flowering' to the housewives. This entailed the giving out of dozens and dozens of fine linen handkerchiefs, which the locals embellished with the most beautiful embroidery. Sitting by candlelight, or at best an oil lamp, the farmers' wives, having gathered in the eggs, bedded their cattle, put the children in their cots and fed their menfolk, sat down to produce their little floral decorations in the corner of the handkerchiefs. The final products were works of art that have yet to be surpassed by anything emanating from the machine or computer age. Later it was found that the Chinese had the same skills but did it more cheaply and this old cottage industry was regrettably lost.

Here in Ballygowan John Henry spent his childhood in a protected, happy atmosphere with no responsibilities resting on his shoulders. In the 1950s he returned about once a year to attend the morning service at the Presbyterian Church. Here the Ballygowan boy who had risen to academic success was greeted by his childhood acquaintances, all eager to speak to him and shake his hand. Later in life when he was heavily burdened with hospital work and administrative decisions he would often recall the idyllic times of his early life in the town and sometimes take his car on a sentimental journey past his early home in the Square and on to Carrickmannon School. From the village life he learned the warm feeling of belonging to a close-knit community where everyone played a part in the team in order to make it work. The humblest were as important as the richest, for the one could not function without the other. He saw the poor struggling to overcome adversity, yet managing to keep smiles on their faces and warmth in their hearts. I do not think that he ever forgot these lessons in human nature as he ascended the ladder of professional success. Whether it was in the Pathology Laboratory or the University he tried to recreate this friendly community atmosphere in which each person took a pride in acting their own little part. In this way he undoubtedly got the best from his loyal followers. Although as he grew older he tended to be regarded with awe by some of his professional colleagues, he always had the time to stop for a chat and share a joke with a hospital porter, a hospital domestic or a shop assistant.

Chapter 2

School days at 'Inst'

In September 1918 John Henry, the 12 year old country boy, travelled from his home in Ballygowan to Belfast on the 7.30am train. He was thrilled as he entered, for the first time, the historic school, the Royal Belfast Academical Institution, better known simply as 'Inst'. This early train got him to school in good time, but he was later to make a deal with his chemistry master that he could arrive ten minutes late for his class without punishment. This enabled him to catch the 8am train so that he could travel accompanied by his dream girl of that particular moment.

Situated in Belfast city centre, the foundation stone of Inst had been laid in 1810 but the building was not ready to admit boys until 1814. Joseph R. Fisher,* Barrister-at-Law, wrote in his introductory historical chapter of the 1810–1910 *Centenary Volume of RBAI*:

> It was in this united and tolerant spirit that the fathers of the Academical Institution met to take up their responsible and important task and to create a centre of free and non-sectarian education which was destined through many good fruit for succeeding generations of Ulstermen.

By the early twentieth century the school had already a remarkable record of educational and sporting achievement. Like most boys, John Henry had had to sit an entrance examination, but always admitted that he had not done himself justice due to an attack of 'butterflies and collywobbles', though he passed comfortably.

It is easy to imagine how this new boy, in his newly acquired plain black cap with its gold initialled monogram, sensed the spirits of former pupils around him as he proudly joined the school. He could hardly believe his

---

* Fisher, J.R.: *R.B.A.I., Centenary Volume*, 1810–1910; 32: 1913, McCaw, Stevenson & Orr, Ltd.

luck to have the opportunity to mingle with future rugby internationals, future scholars at Oxford and Cambridge and exhibitioners at Queen's and Trinity College, Dublin. To him this was the champagne of youth and its effervescence seemed to pervade the whole school.

The Principal at that time was Robert Millar Jones. He was regarded by many of his pupils as a superb and erudite teacher, but although John Henry admired and respected him, he had reservations stemming from the resemblance he bore to his own father – even down to his stiff linen collar and cuffs. He freely admitted that this similarity may have tainted his opinion and over-magnified the disciplinarian image. Yet in later years when 'R.M.' corrected John Henry's translation of Horace from 'bloody seas' to 'seas incarnadine', or his crude description of 'uxor femoris' into 'winsome wife' he began to appreciate the beautiful austerity of the man.

For one day in his school life John Henry remembered regarding R.M. in an altogether more favourable light. The snow was on the ground when Inst was scheduled to play Campbell College in the semi-final of that most titanic of struggles – the Ulster School's Rugby Cup. The ground designated was unplayable and the venue was changed to Bladon Drive – the playing fields of Instonians (Inst's former pupils). Campbell had objected on the basis of neutrality and a cheer rose from the ranks when R.M. arranged to transport the entire school of Inst by bus to Campbell College in support of their team. On yet another occasion, in 1920, the Principal circulated a notice around the school summoning all pupils to assemble immediately in the gymnasium – Form 1 at the front and prefects to take charge. For half an hour the school listened to his eloquent discourse on the state of crime in Ireland. Then in tones equally severe, he continued by stating that in such times it was impossible to prevent the admission of every little guttersnipe to the school, and that one such had recently placed a whole roll of toilet paper in the lavatory, so necessitating the digging up of the quadrangle. In spite of his austerity there was also a sense of stylistic perfection as R.M. led his pupils through Virgil, Livy and Horace imparting to the class the ideal words for the translation.

In John Henry's final year at Inst R.M. advised him that he was attempting to carry too many subjects: as he put it 'It was not possible for men to know all things and that as he was doomed to become a student of medicine he could with advantage give up Greek'. John Henry apparently agreed to his face, but secretly arranged with his Greek teacher that although he attended no classes he would continue to submit a Greek composition each week. R.M. must have wondered how a student, no longer studying the subject, came to be awarded the Hyndman scholarship in Latin and Greek.

R.M. each year invited the prefects to his home at Maryville in the Malone district of Belfast. (At this historic house King William III was reputed to have stabled his horse on the way to his victory at the Boyne). For the delectation of the prefects he had gathered together some of the more presentable young ladies of the Belfast schools. Unlike Methodist College, which was co-educational, Inst boys were ruled with Spartan simplicity, but it was generally accepted that they more than caught up with the Methody boys in the first year after school. Anyhow, this was the first approved outing with the fair sex. Two bowls of flowers were circulated and one's partner for the evening was the young lady whose flower matched that of the boy's. As John Henry had been a prefect for three years, he had rapidly learnt to have a look at what fortune the floral bowl had produced. If she looked 'too Presbyterian', or not so promising as one might have wished, he would persuade some of his unsuspecting juniors that a rose, for example was preferable to a carnation. After one or two such exchanges it was generally possible to disappear accompanied into the garden and escape many of the very sophisticated parlour games that the more recent prefects had to endure.

Yet though R.M. dominated the scene and appeared a remote papal-like figure issuing his edicts, John Henry was later to learn the intense interest he maintained in his former pupils when, as a Queen's Curator, R.M. took him through his past life during the interview for the Chair of Pathology at Queen's.

John Henry felt that he was particularly fortunate to attend Inst at a time when it could boast so many outstanding teachers. Not only were they good teachers and scholars, but most were endowed with a personality which could have made them acceptable for any senior teaching position in Great Britain. None stimulated him or impressed him more than J.C.A. Brierley and Miss M. Kay. They taught him not only the facts of science but also captured his interest as they led him from peak after peak of discovery – Lavoisier to Boyle to Dalton to Röentgen. His knowledge of science grew, but grew in the connotation of the history and philosophy of the subject. This was indeed not simply learning but education at its best. He attributed his own later skills as a teacher of medical students to his using the same methodology which had been so inspirationally instilled by his own teachers at this formative stage in his development. Brierley, however, could never understand why John Henry liked Greek. My father would sometimes mischievously threaten to give up either Science or Greek and then try to sit close to the two appropriate masters at lunch to eavesdrop on their conversation as they ardently defended their subjects.

The Greek master was George Ernest Laurie. He held a first class honours degree in classics from Oxford and was a rugby 'blue'. These qualifications gave him a flying start in the eyes of his pupils and he was generally held in high regard. Of the three or four people whom my father considered to have given a strong sense of direction to his life, Laurie held pride of place. It was Laurie who decided that he should take up Greek, a year after starting at Inst. From September to December he was given the opportunity to complete the whole of *one year's* pass work. In January he was transferred to the honours class taken by Laurie himself and had to learn quickly the requisite physical contortions necessary to escape impact with the large edition of Liddel and Scott – a huge volume which Laurie aimed with accuracy at the head of anyone who did less than justice to the poesy of Homer or Xenophon or failed to appreciate the dramatic potential of Euripides or Aristophanes. It was not the teaching of the actual language that bore the most lasting fruit since my father soon discovered, whilst reading Plato's *Republic*, that a question put to Laurie on philosophy could be more rewarding. If asked such a question Laurie would rise from behind the table, put his hands in his pockets and delight the entire class (only five in number) with his discussion of the Platonic ethic, leading on to the neo-Platonists, and ending with the Stoics and Cicero. John Henry certainly excelled at learning the Greek language with its vocabulary and grammar, but it was the implantation of these philosophical seeds in Laurie's classroom that was to have such a lasting effect when, in later years, he would often ponder deeply on various aspects of life.

George Ernest Laurie was not only the head of the classical department; he also took charge of the rugby teams. In those days rugby at Inst displaced sectarian bitterness and was a religion of its own. The first time John Henry turned out he had never seen a rugby game before and he stuck his head into all sorts of impossible positions in the scrum. Yet within two years he was on the 1st XV. It was a curiously intellectual team – several, including John Henry and Tom Hewitt (an Irish international), entered Queen's University with foundation scholarships, but there were also Ashley Price who could translate Homer unprepared and won a scholarship at Merton College, Oxford; J.K. Barnes an entrance scholarship at Jesus College, Oxford; W.A. Newman, an entrance scholarship at Jesus College, Oxford; and Dave Lindsay, an entrance scholarship at Exeter College, Oxford. All were able to dribble the oval ball and charge as solidly as any Roman phalanx. It remains open to doubt whether such scholarly success in the 1st XV was due to Laurie's like of classical scholars or their athletic ability.

All of this my father owed to Laurie, but it was also he who introduced him to the pleasures of music for the first time by taking him as a schoolboy to the opera, seeing such performances as *La Bohème*, *La Traviata*, and the Gilbert and Sullivan classics. This awakened a love of music which was to be a great solace to him throughout the rest of his life.

Though John Henry loved music and classical art, he claimed that he gave his greatest love to the music of words, to words well chosen to clothe an idea, words that had a cadence of a violin concerto – expressing mind, but expressing it not in a harsh raucous noise, but in the sweet music of perfect selection – the word suiting the mood, and catching the melody and perfection of the thought. He did not know where he acquired this skill, for he inherited it neither from his father nor his mother. It was the head of the English Department, John Bell, who nurtured and cultivated this ability by incorporating into his teaching something of the magic of the language. He was able to turn even the dullest exercise into something of the mystical. It was a great disappointment and personal loss to John Henry when within a short time Bell left Inst to take up a similar appointment at the Royal High School, Edinburgh.

One of the most lovable of the masters was James ('Johnny') Pyper. He was a hard practical Ulsterman keen on accurate knowledge. The dates of events and ordinances were things to be remembered and John Henry could still remember in late life that Pope Julius II had something to do with a crusade in 1492. Pyper took the class for historical geography – a curious subject that seems to have disappeared from the curriculum. He was capable of transmitting all the enthusiasm and fear of the early adventurers as the class sailed with Prince Henry of Portugal, and rounded the Cape with Vasco da Gama.

The Mathematics Department was led by W.H.E. 'Bubbly' Martin, who was so nicknamed because of his tendency to erupt and spray the front rows of his class with multiple tiny bubbles of saliva as he enthusiastically

Mr Harriman's 2nd Form, French class, John Henry seated on left of schoolmaster (1920)

expounded on the problems of the day. Another, H. Sinclair, was cruelly known as 'Boozy' Sinclair on account of his unfortunate puce-coloured nose. The kindest of the mathematicians, however, was J.H.A. 'Theta' Carson, who later generations knew as 'Baldy' Carson. On one occasion my father shocked 'Theta' when an inspector from the Ministry was there, by solving a problem on the blackboard using the old fashioned, but mathematically accurate, 'chain rule'. It was a trick that his father had taught him, but 'Theta' had never seen it used by any previous student. Whether it was because of this incident or not, my father thereafter gained a special place in 'Theta's' affection.

The Head of the Modern Languages Department was Frederick George Harriman (F.G.H.) who in John Henry's early days at school boasted a moustache worthy of the most eminent officer in the R.A.F. One day he appeared fully shorn and cleanly shaven and invited a member of the class to translate 'La Joie fait peur'. The student, a large man, subsequently to become a professor of Chemistry, calmly raised his eyebrows and said: 'And who are you?' Harriman was considered by my father to be a most approachable and lovable man although it was only later that he came to recognise his full value.

Other contemporaries included 'Black Jack' and 'Coppernob' or 'Cop' McKenna, 'spring-heeled Jack' Cowser, 'Hendy' Henderson and 'Beaky'

Manning – all of them had something to give and gave it warmly and with a great sense of humanity.

It was possible to obtain a remarkable breadth of education at Inst in those days. Never was there the faintest indication of 'cramming' for examinations. There was a great breadth to it all, no limitation to two or three subjects in the Upper Sixth. It was possible to pursue as many subjects as one wanted thus providing a large pedestal of general knowledge on which to build one's future life. There was plenty of homework, and a full realisation that the more one put into life and knowledge, the more could be gained from it. So eventually John Henry was to leave school with the Sullivan Scholarship in Mathematics, the Hyndman Scholarship in Latin and Greek, the Musgrave Scholarship in French (its first award), the Blain Memorial Scholarship in History, and a Queen's University Entrance Foundation Scholarship in Physics and Chemistry. This list sounds like the achievement of an academic swot, but far from it. The academia was more than balanced by his attainments in other spheres of school activities. He was on the 1st XV for three years winning honours caps in 1922 and 1923 and earning an Ulster School's rugby honours cap in 1923, was a prefect for three years, a competent member of the Debating Society, played soccer for Ballygowan in the Summer League, and in general lived a thoroughly full and enjoyable life.

RBAI 1st XV. Those in white jerseys have represented Ulster schoolboys XV.
John Henry is one of these seated to the right. The other Ulster players
are all from the famous Hewitt family (1923)

Chapter 3

A preclinical student at Queen's University

Arrival at Queen's University in 1923 from Upper Sixth at Inst was not such a transition for my father as it was for many students from other local schools. In the Upper Sixth (the final year) at Inst the practice of seeking sources of knowledge on one's own had been positively encouraged though the teachers were, however, always available for consultation when necessary. This was essentially the relationship practised by John Henry and his teachers who discussed problems, often far removed from the syllabus, as if between equals. Indeed troubles only arose when John Henry and his pals were caught in the handball alley after stealing out of the Physics laboratory window. In the early nineteen-twenties Queen's was a university with the blessing of scarcely two thousand students in attendance and it was possible to talk in the Students' Union with budding classicists, modern linguists, embryo lawyers, chemists and physicists, biologists and economists. In those days the medical school was the dominant faculty. Throughout Northern Ireland, but perhaps more particularly in County Antrim, there were certain traditions in the farming community: one son inherited the farm; another entered the church, whilst another frequently studied medicine. The captains of school rugby, the scholarship boys, and indeed more often than not the cream of the Ulster grammar schools were often to be found in the medical school. In John Henry's time each President of the Students' Representative Society, including himself, was a medical student. Of course the Medical Faculty was the largest in the University, and by reason of its much longer curriculum, held within its ranks older and *hopefully* more mature students. This dominance has been corrected by the great expansion of the other faculties in recent years.

In his first year at Queen's John Henry faced two new subjects, botany and zoology. In botany, James Small, the professor, introduced his first lecture: 'Ladies and Gentlemen *and medical students*', and having thus thrown down the gauntlet to the majority of the class he was forced to fight for his survival as teacher and lecturer for the remainder of the course. The medical students almost always successfully outmanoeuvred him, but even my father was stricken with some remorse for him when one, Davidson from Omagh, presented him at the end of the course with a bouquet of dandelions. During the course Professor Small's wife happened to advertise for a housekeeper and unwisely gave her name and address. She received some seventy applications all originating from Queen's medical students. When John Henry became Dean of the Faculty of Medicine in 1943, he discovered that Small was failing up to 75% of the first year medical class. Seemingly John Henry threatened to withdraw botany as a subject in the first year curriculum as the days of herbalism were thought to be over and the advent of evidence-based clinical therapeutics and pharmacology was already signalled. Small was very emotionally disturbed by this suggestion for, although he felt justified in regarding the medical students as fodder, due to their numbers, the very existence of his department largely depended on them. John Henry was thereafter promised that if he withdrew the threat no future medical student would have to suffer the ignominy of failing botany. John Henry agreed and throughout Jimmy Small's final years in post he hardly ever failed a medical student, although the students were never made aware of the truth behind their easy passage through the botanical wonderland. They continued to buy Small's textbook and try to understand the osmosis of the root of the bean.

Zoology does not seem to have fired my father with any great enthusiasm; he thought it was taught in an unimaginative manner, although acquisition of its vocabulary was to be a help to him in future years. The professor (Gregg Wilson) was a strict disciplinarian, and woe betides any of his students who appeared before him on the University Discipline Committee, as on one occasion John Henry did. In his biographical notes he recounts that:

> Students' Rag Day in 1926 ended with a fancy dress ball in the Great Hall, and I was one of the organising committee. At the end of the Hall was a settee of matrons, wives of professors and Pro-Chancellors, in all a most decorous group, whose boredom the students hoped to keep at bay with presentations of bouquets, boxes of chocolates and the occasional sacrifice of a dance. As a member of the committee I felt some degree of conscience and responsibility for student behaviour. Students had been collecting for charity all day. They had survived attacks in the spinning mills and factories, which they had

daringly invaded. Managers and their staff in the offices of our then more frequent distilleries had poured out generous samples of their wares hoping soon to be left in peace. Girl students had done honour to the night, dressing up as Queens of Sheba and Belles from the Wild West to add beauty and excitement. I felt my first duty was to remove a student who had decided that he did not like a portrait of a former and no doubt eminent professor of philosophy and had shown his dislike by boxing the portrait. Next there was the student who was intent in spending the evening in the Ladies' lavatory. Then the dental student who took what was normally a colourful professor by the lapels of his evening jacket and enquired about the whereabouts of 'the bloody red shirt' that he usually wore. On the whole it was a series of relatively minor incidents. Yet in the morning when I returned to Queen's, the night activities had attained the dimensions of a catastrophe. Rumour grew apace; the Queen of Sheba was the centre of attraction – had the straps of her dress not broken at a critical moment in the cloisters? And had she not fled naked to the waist to the women's quarters pursued by those still able to run? The organising committee for the dance was quickly summoned before the discipline committee.

John Henry and his fellow committee members were interviewed by the deans of all the faculties and grilled about the misbehaviour of students in such situations. Apparently the inquisitors revealed remarkably fervid imaginations. It was only when the final interrogator, the Dean of the Faculty of Medicine, Professor Symmers, asked him 'Biggart, did you see anything that a drop of drink couldn't explain?' that John Henry realised that here at least was a man with his feet on the ground and that the Freudian atmosphere pursued up to that moment was more a reflection upon the deans rather on a fairly inebriated student body. Many years later John Henry took delight in teasing these eminent classicists, zoologists and economists about such things. Some were then prepared to admit that they had over-reacted. Based on this incident, John Henry always said that he gained an inner confidence by realising that a medical training provided an insight and understanding of the range of acceptable human behaviour – an insight not always acquired by the more cloistered academic in his ivory tower.

Alfred Walter Stewart was Professor of Chemistry, and whilst undoubtedly able, he was, unfortunately, nearly deaf. So when he ducked his head down and closely read his script to the class there was often bedlam. It was only years later that his students came to realise that, under the pen name of J.J.

Connington, he was a popular writer of detective stories. Unfortunately for his medical students the space below each row of seats was open to the store beneath the lecture theatre, and there John Carroll, a technician and ex-member of the Royal Irish Constabulary, could easily identify the seat numbers of the more riotous. My father remembered with glee cutting the cords attached to hydrogen-filled balloons which then gently floated towards the ceiling. Still, unlike many of his successors, Professor Stewart did have the courage to lecture to the medical students who, in spite of often being undisciplined and boisterous, held him in high regard.

The chemistry practical was the only examination in which John Henry ever attained 100% even though his carefully weighed platinum crucible of potassium chlorate had sparked considerably over the bench. He later admitted to attaining this exceptional mark by the indirect means of knowing the chemical formula and applying his mathematical skills to evaluate what the correct percentage loss of oxygen should be, rather than by weighing the spluttering specimen.

The teacher in the first year who impressed him most was William Blair Morton, the Professor of Physics. In beautiful English he expounded the problems of his subject, holding the interest of the unruly medical students by a generous injection of humour. He seemed to revel in making complicated concepts appear simple. He was an outstanding after-dinner speaker, widely regarded, and at the Charter Day luncheons and dinners he titillated the intellectual palates of his audience with a choice epigram or a little teasing of 'the powers that be', stilling criticism and avoiding offence by his cheerful whimsical delivery. My father had no knowledge of his standing as a physicist, but as a teacher he had no doubt that he made the first medical year worthwhile. He also profited from it since he gained first place and first class honours in both physics and chemistry.

With their first year studies, seeming so distant from their chosen profession of medicine, behind them, the students felt that at long last they were to face subjects of more obvious relevance, viz. anatomy, biochemistry and physiology. There was, however, a tradition that there should be one last fleeting and disrespectful visit to the department of botany. So, armed with various missiles, John Henry and his colleagues filled the lecture theatre on the first day of the new term to set the standards of behaviour for students of subsequent years. (This ritual was still practised in the mid-1950s when I was a medical student at Queen's. However, I was rather more timorous in participating in the rowdy behaviour as my father was now Dean of the Medical Faculty and I was completely in the dark about his own Richard Gordon-type behaviour in the 1920s). Such rowdy behaviour by medical students had occurred in the past and Professor Small, forewarned and forearmed, informed the assembled miscreants that all exits were manned by university porters; names would be taken and all the powers of the University authority would be deployed against them. Uproar ensued and the missiles were duly propelled. Fortunately, the professor had forgotten that his retiral room had a separate staircase. My father and friends cascaded over the rostrum and through the sacred anteroom to emerge from the private staircase into the unmanned safety of the quadrangle.

In their second year John Henry and his fellow-students met an entirely different breed of teacher. In physiology there was Professor Tommy Milroy, a courteous Edwardian who promulgated his subject at a high scientific level. He and his brother John, who became the first professor of biochemistry, were charming men, who pursued their research quietly and without ostentation. They gained the affection of the medical students with their 'Old World' courtesy.

Medical students in those days, in spite of their 'short back and sides' and their conformity with their elders in dress, were possibly a tougher breed of men than those of today. Many had been First World War soldiers, who had had it tough in the trenches and were prepared to be tough in return. They came back from the war hell-bent and led younger students like my father into some escapades – some clever and well designed, some not so clever and some disastrous. Many of the great university rags of that time were the products of their ingenuity, particularly those greeting William Massey, Prime Minister of New Zealand, and Winston Churchill, when they were given honorary degrees.

My father was greatly impressed by the lectures from the Professor of Anatomy, Thomas Walmsley, a Scot who, though a man of the Borders, had been influenced by his early years in India. He had not served in the war and so one day the sanctity of the rostrum was invaded and he found himself, gown and all, immersed in a pond in the adjacent Botanic Gardens. Yet he survived this inauspicious beginning and gradually became accepted and was the philosophic gnome of the faculty. John Henry revelled in his lectures as he skilfully succeeded in weaving together the hard facts of anatomy and the philosophy of the subject. Difficult things were made simple, but not oversimplified. Many years later, when John Henry was trying to understand the structure and function of the hypothalamus in the brain, he said he was still able to remember the scientifically clear way that he had been introduced to the third ventricle of the brain. There were also excursions to the Belfast Medical Students' Association where he enthralled them with a discourse on 'A Basket of Bones'. He was a great teacher with a reserved personality. He succeeded in stimulating many of the best students to return to anatomy for their lifetime careers, and attaining chairs in many parts of the world. Two of these, William James Hamilton and James Dixon Boyd were amongst the leading anatomists in the world.

Yet possibly all the credit for the success of the Anatomy Department should not be attributed to Walmsley, for back from the USA in the early twenties came as his lecturer one of the great characters of the contemporary Belfast medical scene – one Dr Richard Hunter (better known as 'Dicky'). He had taken up medicine after a period in business, after acting as an interpreter for the British troops in France, and partly because his brother, a general practitioner, had died from pneumonia after an exhausting journey in the snow to reach one of his patients. Author, actor, artist, he brought to the subject of embryology a feeling of adventure. Though a lifelong bachelor, he was to my father's contemporaries the ultimate authority on procreation. From semen to ovum to blastocyst, to embryo to foetus they followed his magic drawings and his wit. He had the great facility of knowing each and every one of his students.

As a sideline 'Dicky' acted as pathologist to the Belfast zoo and from this developed his attachment to the circus. In the summer vacation he often toured the eastern towns of England with the Chipperfield Circus. Clad in his scarlet coat and top hat he acted as ringmaster. Indeed when I was a young boy in the 1940s he was still playing this role at the annual Christmas circus in Belfast at the Royal Hippodrome theatre, which then stood adjacent to the Grand Opera House. In full evening dress in 1937 at the British Medical Association Meeting in Belfast he entered the lions' cage at the zoo, armed only with a broom and put many of the medical worthies in danger of regurgitating the ample hospitality they had enjoyed. He was eventually persuaded to give up anatomy for the administrative post of Secretary of Queen's University, in which role he was again to hit up an influential relationship when my father returned as Professor of Pathology and later as Dean of the Faculty of Medicine. I shall return to this in a subsequent chapter.

In anatomy the medical students worked in pairs in the dissecting room and John Henry was doomed, or fortunate, according to how one looked at it, to have two partners who subsequently became professors of that subject. As he recalls it, in his first year at anatomy his partner 'W.J.' (probably William James Hamilton) was an enthusiastic dissector. My father truly believed that W.J. would be disappointed if he were deprived by his absence of removing even a single globule of fatty tissue. Thus John Henry decided to let him do all the major dissection, whilst he departed to the Students' Union for a game of billiards. Every hour, though, John Henry would return to the dissecting room and there he would find that W.J. had exposed artery, vein, nerve and muscle even more beautifully than in the text book illustrations. In a few moments John Henry had gained more appreciation of the problem than the dissector who had laboured lovingly and tenderly for so long. So after a little look and a little reading he returned to the billiard room. This pattern continued for two years.

In his second year John Henry's partner, (possibly James Dixon Boyd, Hamilton's colleague) was also to become a Professor of Anatomy. He remembered returning from one of the sporting sessions in the Students' Union to point out to his dissecting partner, who had just removed the brain, that he had succeeded in cutting the 'bloody' third nerve. Suddenly a voice behind him enquired whether he knew the symptoms of a man who had fallen from a great height but had fallen on his feet. Turning round he realised that the professor had overheard his remark and he had to listen patiently as he explained how the man might be semiconscious and if disturbed might be particularly liable to swear. My father took the point and at least temporarily curbed his language, before again hastening off once more to the billiard hall. That year all his practice was rewarded when he won the University billiard championship. What gave him real pleasure, however, was to win in the same year the Symington Medal in Anatomy, thus confounding the educational theories of the professor. It was the first year of its award.

In the last week of term there was something of a contretemps with Mr Harry Malcolm, (then assistant surgeon at the Royal Victoria Hospital and a part-time lecturer in applied anatomy) who taught the lymphatic drainage and surface anatomical markings. He was a most beautiful draughtsman with blackboard chalks and usually, when the students entered, the board was artistically adorned. As the lecture progressed these drawings had to be erased and replaced by equally decorous ones. On this occasion, as John

Henry well remembered, the imp within him, usually kept suppressed, led him to hide the blackboard duster. He was sitting on it when the critical moment of Malcolm, realising its absence, arrived. Threats there were and it was obviously too late to confess, so the lecturer stomped out of the theatre. Suddenly he returned to find John Henry on top of the bench urging the other students to do likewise. Caught red handed, he was unceremoniously ejected. One week later John Henry had to face Malcolm in the second professional examination. Malcolm's co-examiner was 'Dicky' Hunter who greeted my father as the recent winner of the Symington Medal whilst Harry Malcolm recognised him as the malcontent who had disturbed the peace and order of his lecture. The outcome of this *viva* in applied anatomy established in my father's mind the general fairness of examiners, for though he knew little about lymphatic drainage apart from general principles, he was still awarded a high mark in spite of being in Malcolm's 'dog-house'; and he was placed first with first class honours in anatomy in the 2nd M.B. examination. He described Malcolm as a charming man who subsequently developed many neat effective orthopaedic techniques. He was popular with women but somehow never won a companion for himself.

Firmly embedded in John Henry' memory was his physiology *viva*. He and a fellow-student were sitting in chairs only a few yards away from a rather hot-tempered external examiner, but they could easily hear the interrogation of the student immediately in front of them. As my father sat he heard the victim being asked some question or other, to which he obviously gave an unacceptable reply as the extern examiner exploded: 'My God, man, where did you learn that?' The student was heard to respond: 'Thou shalt not take the name of the Lord in vain'. Once more there was an explosion and the rapid exit of the student. So it was with some trepidation that John Henry moved towards the hot chair. His first question was about the method of oxygen transfer in the lung, and having given the usually accepted theories he ventured to mention a possible secretory function for the cells lining the air spaces. Again an explosion. But John Henry assured the irate professor that those eminent physiologists, Starling, Bayliss and Menzies, and indeed his own professor, discussed such a possibility. Since the extern had possibly not consulted such textbooks in years, he was on a relatively poor wicket and the ordeal terminated on relatively friendly terms.

Thus he succeeded by ability and a certain amount of quick-minded agility to convince his teachers that he was more than ready to jump the hurdle of the Second Professional Examination to reach the fascination of the clinical subjects that lay ahead. He was obviously relishing the freedom of the academic environment and able, with his retentive memory, to absorb the necessary knowledge whilst participating fully in the available leisure activities and even at times exhibiting the 'high jinks' considered by those who disapprove to be so typical of medical students. In defence of the latter it must be recognised that such behaviour could be explained as a relatively harmless 'escape valve' for the stress induced by the amount and depth of knowledge that was and is still expected of those studying medicine.

Chapter 4

A clinical student

Having surmounted the hurdle of the Second Professional Examination, John Henry and his student colleagues proceeded to hospital, most to the Royal Victoria. Spending their mornings at hospital they would dash back to the Students' Union on the main University campus for lunch prior to a full afternoon of lectures on site. At that time there were few, if any, cars amongst the students and the journey by tramcar was tedious, so they either cycled or walked and chatted about their morning experiences. For the first time they felt that they were becoming engaged in their profession: after all they had entered the medical school to become doctors, although just exactly what that meant to them was difficult to define. For most it meant something to do with patients and their ailments, but as my father noted 'we had a rather mystical conception of what a doctor could do'. On the whole, however, they were prepared to give more to life than they expected to gain from it – a healthy, enthusiastic band of boys and girls who worked hard and knew how to enjoy themselves. In hospital they were well taught by Cecil Calvert, Ian Fraser, Cecil Woodside and George McFadden who introduced them to the elementary clinical surgical problems. John Henry admitted that 'one of the greatest difficulties was overcoming his shyness of bodily and physical intimacy'. As a boy of twenty he found it difficult to deal with a middle-aged female patient unburdening herself of all her marital worries and sexual problems. He also felt shy at the degree of physical exposure necessary to make a complete clinical examination. Yet slowly and almost subconsciously by frequent repetition of such tasks he and the other medical students became more confident and learned the art of taking a medical history, gradually realising that this could be the most important element in the diagnosis of a patient's illness.

John Henry considered these afternoon lectures on the university campus something of a slog. Most of the lecturers, many of whom were part-time, lacked the ability of firing the students with enthusiasm, but to him there was one notable exception – Professor Symmers, Professor of Pathology, who stood head and shoulders above the rest. Not only was he Dean of the Medical Faculty, but my father always considered him to be its most cultured member. A lecture on parasites could easily evolve into a discussion 'likely to take us to W. H. Hudson's "Purple Land,"' and his audience could become lost in dreams and visions of South America. He seemingly made pathology so attractive that ever afterwards no other medical subject gave John Henry a similar intellectual reward. Symmers was an excellent Greek scholar and possessed a most beautiful edition of Plato which my father would have loved to buy after Symmers' death, if only his finances had permitted.

The Professor of Materia Medica and Therapeutics (John Elder MacIlwaine) gave them sure guidance, but the subject as then taught was dull as ditch-water which doomed him from the start in the students' eyes. John Henry thought that the lecturer in pharmacology, E.B.C. 'Physo' Mayrs, resembled *The Doctor* in Samuel Luke Fylde's well known painting, (bearded and seated and solemnly pondering at the bedside of a very sick child), but unfortunately his appearance belied his personality and he had no sense of humour. A previous year's class had apparently brought a donkey and cart through the door of his practical class by removing the wheels. They then reassembled the cart, without replacing the wheel pins, so when 'Physo' arrived and tried to lead the donkey out through the doorway the contraption collapsed. The lecturer, donkey, cart and its contents ended in some confusion on the floor. With this and other pranks in the unwritten legends of the Faculty, it was not surprising that he was regarded as fair game by each successive generation of students. In my father's year he was demonstrating the proper method of adding a few minims of a potent drug to a bottle of medicine when a small bomb, then used by motor cyclists of the time to fend off following dogs, exploded on the blackboard behind him. Then with arms extended and with black gown floating like a raven's wings, he poured not six drops, but a generous splash into his preparation as he fled the room.

It was a lecture theatre rich in such history. My father recorded that on one occasion students paid an organ-grinder and his monkey to play outside the window during the lecture. The lecture began and the organ-grinder immediately started to play as the monkey cavorted on the windowsill. Porters were sent for but the organ-grinder insisted in fulfilling his contract with the young *gentlemen.* He had been paid for the hour and an hour's music he would give. One student, later to become a consultant, expressed his enjoyment of the situation so enthusiastically that he was ejected from the lecture and sent outside to join his little friend at the window.

John Henry, from his entry into Queen's, became involved in student politics and showed an avid interest in administration. He immediately became the representative of his year on the Students' Representative University Council (SRC), a body whose constitution had been based very largely on that of the Scottish Universities. Unlike most English Universities, the President, if a graduate of the University, had a seat (and of course a vote) on the Senate, which in Queen's is the sovereign body equivalent to the Council in most English universities; if not a graduate he/she could be invited to be 'in attendance'. Eventually John Henry became SRC auditor and returning officer before being elected its President in 1927. Indeed in those days the Presidents invariably came from the Faculty of Medicine. This was not as unusual as it might seem, for the medical students had a five-year curriculum and became senior students in spite of themselves. The immediately preceding Presidents had been John Beattie (later Professor of Anatomy at McGill University), then Bernard Barne (who became Professor at the Royal College of Surgeons), and Hugh Gault Calwell, a distant relative of my father, who after a distinguished career in the colonial medical service, returned to his homeland to introduce the Mass Radiography Service and finally became Honorary Archivist at the Royal Victoria Hospital.

In his year as President of SRC an effort was made to revise its constitution. Weekly committee meetings were held in which he was greatly assisted by George B. Hanna, subsequently King's Counsel and a Minister in the local parliament at Stormont. Hanna was a great raconteur and my father later used some of his stories to enliven an after-dinner speech, especially when the audience was entirely male. When, as President, John Henry encountered any little administrative problems, he would seek advice and help from the Dean of the Medical Faculty, Professor Symmers. The Dean would take him to see the University Bursar or the Secretary and quickly resolve the matter that was engendering so much paper work, by informing these officers that they were making a mountain out of a molehill. This was a principle that John Henry readily absorbed and put to frequent use in his later administrative life. He was also, during his clinical student years, to hold the offices of Vice-President of the Students' Union and Vice-President of the Belfast Medical Students' Association.

During his term of office as President of SRC, John Henry introduced the immunity badge for students' rag day. There was much opposition and a mass meeting of students. He pointed out that the issue of badges was limited to one thousand and that as the city had a population of about 300,000 a sufficient supply of 'virgin lips' were likely to be encountered. The SRC Committee also prevailed on the Vice Chancellor, Sir Richard Livingstone, to depute certain disciplinary powers to the student body, and actually no students had to appear before the University Discipline Committee during my father's year of office. The evening dance that year was held for the first time outside the precincts of the University, in the Plaza Ballroom in Chichester Street in downtown Belfast, and passed without serious incident.

In addition to the annual rag day for charitable causes, there were other 'rags' involving famous visitors to the city and new appointees to the University Chairs. The tradition largely centred on the medical school and rags organised by other faculties tended to be relatively damp squibs. In John Henry's first year (1923) there was the traditional introduction for Professor C.G. Lowry in Obstetrics, Professor W.W.D. Thomson in Medicine, and Professor Andrew 'Andy' Fullerton in Surgery. C.G. Lowry had to ride a donkey bareback down to the centre of the city and it was doubtful if he ever forgave the students for the trauma to his perineum. W.W.D. Thomson and Andy Fullerton were captured between lectures, dressed in their pyjamas, gowns and mortarboards, taken to the City Hall and appropriately anointed. They rode in a brougham drawn by long ropes manned by students. Apparently the expression on the face of the police points-man on duty at the corner of May Street was a sight to be seen, when he held up his hand to stop the rapidly approaching brougham and found that the ropes had already passed him. He saved himself only by jumping on to one of the shafts of the cart.

But the great rags of John Henry's student days were those in 1923 for William Ferguson Massey, Prime Minister of New Zealand (1912–25) but of Ulster lineage and formerly from Limavady, and in 1926 for Winston Churchill. Somewhat later was that for Sir Thomas Houston, the benevolent initiator of Clinical Pathology in Belfast. For Massey, my father and his fellow students had adorned themselves as Maoris and a great ceremonial feast was held on the front lawn of the University. He was then conducted downtown to the Ulster Reform Club, but on the way back the student ranks were broken and a girl's school invaded. Many of the young maidens had their cheeks smudged by the stain from the students' darkened complexions. My father was overcome by remorse for the ruffled girls when he heard them being reproved by their lady teacher. So to make things fair and equal he besmirched her cheeks as well. Besmirched or not, she subsequently became Head Mistress of St Leonard's in St Andrews, Scotland.

Winston Churchill was granted an honorary degree in 1926, and when he eventually emerged from the Senate luncheon, he was seized by the students, crowned with an Irish paddy hat with green ribbon, given a white clay pipe and placed in an Irish jaunting car. Before him marched a cohort of 'Hibernians', suitably bedecked, with John Henry in charge. Behind him came the paramilitary 'Ulster Volunteers' including 'the Rising Sons of Belial' under the charge of George B. Hanna, blue-suited, belted, and armed with wooden replica rifles. The procession marched to the Ulster Hall, to which Winston had been denied access in 1912 since it had already been occupied by the Ulster Volunteer Force. Then the 'Hibernians' led him through the Hall and out through the rear door, where he found the 'Ulster Volunteer Force' lined up for his inspection. Winston entered into the spirit of the occasion enjoying the subtlety of it all. With his panache for hats and other strange garbs he was photographed some weeks later at a race meeting wearing his recently acquired paddy hat.

Then there was Sir Thomas Houston encased in knightly armour overcoming the sixty-foot dragon. The students had the greatest difficulty in finding a suit to fit him and unfortunately every time he tried to speak the visor of his helmet fell with a clang and his burly moustache must have scarcely escaped amputation. However, he eventually slew the dragon, and the twenty or so students who had constituted its internal engine gratefully spilled out into Arthur Square.

These were the initial rags, which were to set a precedent to be continued down the years. Each new professor's sense of humour was tested by his 'rag' and, if found wanting, his popularity would dip and his students would no longer be the quiet recipients of his knowledge. In later years, unfortunately, 'rags' came to be less well planned and to centre too closely on the relationship of the new professor's tolerance of alcohol. They eventually petered out in the early 1970s when the police considered that the student disguises could provide cover for politically motivated terrorists.

Meantime, John Henry's clinical studies continued. All the ward chiefs at that time were part-timers, giving their services free to the hospital and, as he put it, 'I suppose earning their eventual rewards by impressing the next generation of general practitioners', who would of course in turn repay them by referring their (fee-paying) patients to their favourite hospital consultant. Even the clinical professors (of Medicine, Surgery, Midwifery, Gynaecology, and Materia Medica and Therapeutics) were part-time, paid then (1923–28) the munificent sum of £233 per annum for their official lecture course. Even the title 'professor' brought little reward as the general public regarded each and every consultant as one of this ilk (or, in typical Belfast dialect – *a perfesser*). The students quickly learned to distinguish those who could and would teach and those who couldn't and wouldn't. 'On the whole, however,' my father continued, 'their record of endeavour was very good, in some cases better than that of some of their full-time successors' – those appointed under the joint NHS/QUB arrangements post World War II.

At first, each student was attached to an individual unit, but as the years passed there was much more freedom of movement. Whilst certificates had to be earned in each of the smaller specialities, certain general medical and surgical clinics were packed and others sparsely attended. A story was circulating in John Henry's time that the previous Professor of Medicine had decided to teach on a patient suffering from disease of the aortic valve in the heart. The students, who seemingly had some doubts as to their efficiency with the stethoscope, had planned a deception by all agreeing to make a diagnosis of *mitral valve* disease when asked by the professor to examine the patient. After the first few students had made this diagnosis, the professor hastily re-applied his stethoscope before calling down two more students, but they supported the contrived diagnosis. So the students came down two by two until eventually the whole class were in agreement about the diagnosis. The professor, giving way to this form of Gallup Poll, taught for the remainder of the hour on *mitral stenosis*.

One of the great traditions of Irish medical teaching is the residential pupilship. In 1820 the first medical student pupil was taken into the Frederick Street Hospital, the predecessor of the Royal Victoria Hospital. Unconsciously, he was the embryonic beginning of the Belfast Medical School, for although Inst had already appointed a professor of anatomy (then in the Faculty of Arts!) in 1818, its Faculty of Medicine was not established until 1835. Ever since, the resident pupilship became an important facet of undergraduate training. The pupil was resident in the hospital; his quarters were close to those of the house officers; he was available for service twenty-four hours a day; and though he found solace in unauthorised suppers in the ward kitchen with the night nurses, he was in effect an apprentice house officer. He kept the notes for his patients, performed the simpler laboratory tests, and became adept at catheterisation and the passing of stomach tubes. He did the blood counts, examined the test meals and became proficient with the syringe and the needle. In some, if not all, the surgical units he even gave the anaesthetics. On a rota basis he worked in the casualty department, where on a Friday or Saturday night it could be a very maturing experience. The old political troubles of Ireland were still alight in the 1920s (not surprising for those of us living into the third millennium), so gunshot wounds and drunks could often keep the pupil engaged until the small hours of the morning. My father could remember careering round the extern trying to complete a suture initiated in the scalp of someone who had imbibed too copiously. Yet at that time the number of pupilships was limited. It was not then an official General Medical Council requirement but a hospital tradition. So there was an examination that resulted in the selection of a few who regarded themselves as lucky indeed to be exposed to two months' really hard work.

As John Henry recalled, on his first morning in surgery he was placed on the anaesthetist's stool and gave three anaesthetics for some abdominal complaints. He had never given an anaesthetic before. The surgeon would not allow him to touch the patient's cornea to ascertain whether he was sufficiently unconscious for his reflexes to have been abolished. So he sat and watched the respiration of the patient and gauged the effectiveness of the anaesthetic by the tension used on the abdominal retractors and the temper of the surgeon.

Urea in his ward was a panacea for all things. Hernia operations were dusted with it and few surgical wounds escaped its application. John Henry could find nothing in his surgical textbooks to justify its use. On enquiry from his surgical chief he was told of the experience of that great anatomist, G. Elliot Smith. Apparently travelling in the Middle East, Elliot Smith came upon a Bedouin tent harbouring a patient with a compound fracture of the femur. He had had no medical treatment yet the injured flesh presented as a clean, ruddy granulation tissue. Elliot Smith found the condition difficult to understand but on questioning, the Arab pointed to the she-ass in the corner of the tent, and had daily washed the wound with her urine. And so what was good enough for Mohammed was good enough for Belfast and, without further scientific study, urine was accepted as the panacea. Actually, subsequent physiological investigations might have offered some support for this empirical and historical treatment. This was 'Pa' Kirk, as he was nicknamed, at his best, and over the next year or so John Henry found him most fertile in original ideas though with a complete lack of self-criticism.

John Henry's month as a pupil in the medical wards was not so exciting. The assistant physician in the unit was Dr Stanley Ireland Turkington who was one of the characters of the school. He was primarily interested in diseases of the chest and to watch and listen to 'the Turk' percuss a chest was an experience not to be forgotten. 'Having made up his mind what was wrong, he then proceeded to demonstrate beautifully and convincingly, the sounds that ought to emanate from his diagnosis', whether it was lobar pneumonia or bronchopneumonia or a cavitation of the lung or air in the pleural cavity.

The 'Turk' had gone into medicine to acquire the money to enable him to write. Yet medicine charmed him. He was like a character from *Pickwick Papers*, and my father remembered with admiration and affection his speeches at the Medical Staff dinners – jewels of humour, scintillating with a quiet mordant wit, pointed with classical aphorism. He was a literary man who, being a bachelor, could pursue his hobbies deep into the night. Years later he was to use the professor of pathology as his medical consultant, summoning him to his ward rounds. The clinical history of the patient was examined in detail, the clinical signs demonstrated in 'the Turk's' inimitable way, and the problem posed. John Henry found it intriguing to help him off the fence of differential diagnosis and to point out how the laboratory could help in this, the ultimate stage of decision. Whatever value it was to him, such consultation was a great stimulation to the pathologist, who at some time in the future would have to stand or fall when the ultimate exposure in the mortuary proclaimed the truth. In all my father's medical appointments 'the Turk' was the only physician who used a pathologist in this way and realised that pathologists were interested in the living vital process rather than only in the dead. He found this attitude more prevalent amongst surgeons and enjoyed the same relationship with Cecil Calvert, the first of the neurosurgeons at the Royal. There was a mutual exchange of knowledge with Calvert teaching John Henry much neurology, and John Henry keeping Calvert up to date with the rapidly advancing research in neuropathology.

Then there was Dr S. Boyd Campbell who seemed to take a special interest in my father throughout his student years, though my father never knew the reason but suspected that it was because both families stemmed from North Antrim. Certainly, he always befriended John Henry throughout his life, and in return my father was occasionally able to mollify his colleagues and to help him to get his own way for he was a man who, in his colleague, Dr T.H. Crozier's words, could 'put his case strongly but not always tactfully', and if he disliked a colleague 'he disliked him with every breath that passed his strangled glottis'. Spontaneously kind and generous, my father had much affection for him. He was one of the clinical examiners in Final Medicine. In that exam, John Henry was faced with a patient suffering from some sort of valvular disease of the heart which he claimed to be the relatively rare Austin Flint murmur. My father continues

> The actual examiner was a lady physician, whom I knew was somewhat deaf. She listened to the heart sounds, and could not or would not confirm my diagnosis and appealed to her co-examiner (S. Boyd Campbell). He listened and did not deny the presence of my murmur, but somehow I have always felt, that, when I caught the twinkle in his eye, he too was fooling my examiner.

In the Surgery Finals, John Henry received a prior 'tip' that his case was a child with a tuberculous ulcer. Such 'tipping' was, and still is prevalent, often emanating from kindly nurses who did not like to see their potential future husbands stumbling at the last post. However the practice could be highly dangerous and was often more of a hindrance than a help. My father quickly concluded that he was dealing with a typical case of congenital syphilis, and both examiners agreed with him that the cause of the ulceration was unknown.

So the Final Exam dragged on till on the last day he had his oral examination in Obstetrics and Gynaecology. He knew that he had got off on the wrong foot with his examiner, Professor C.G. Lowry, who started by stating baldly that he had done his residential obstetrical training in the wrong hospital. John Henry was the last student on Lowry's examinee list and the professor was obviously tired. He told him to pick a specimen and talk on anything he thought fit. John Henry sensed disinterest and saw his hoped-for Honours Degree floating out of the window. Honours degrees have always been reserved for a very select group in the Medical Faculty at

Queen's and my father's expectations were clearly to become a member of this group. His predictions, however, proved unfounded and he gained Second Class Honours M.B., B.Ch. B.A.O. together with Bill Basset, James Deeny, Eileen Hill and Harold Lindsay. However two of his mates, Arthur Alexander and Fred Kane gained a very rare First Class Honours. There was no doubt that he was disappointed since he felt that he had been deprived of top honours, even of overall first place, by professional prejudice and examiner's fatigue. However this may have been, the more likely reason for his disappointment was that he had become used to being at the top of the tree and John Henry did not take kindly to coming second in any part of his life. He had therefore on reflection to console himself with having attained first place and First Class Honours in Pathology and Bacteriology, the Adami Medal in Pathology, first place and First Class Honours in Hygiene, runner-up in the Sinclair Medal in Surgery (oh dear), and the Gold Medal of the Ulster Hospital for Diseases of Children (back on course). A slip to third place in Materia Medica (now known as Therapeutics and Pharmacology) helped to display that he was only human.

Chapter 5

Young doctor in training

Suddenly the protective mesh of 'cotton wool', which had sheltered the medical student in the University environment, was gone and John Henry found himself stepping gingerly on to the first rung of a new ladder of opportunity. He found it an exciting but daunting challenge. It was time to test his theoretical clinical knowledge and put it into practice. Whilst he had high hopes of gaining an appointment as a House Officer in the Royal Victoria Hospital, such an appointment was two months off.

For a time he did holiday relief in the Ulster Hospital for Children and Women situated at that time at Templemore Avenue in the east of the city. One Sunday morning the midwife called him out to see a woman already in labour but not progressing. He examined her as he had been taught and advised the application of an abdominal binder to bring her pendulous abdomen to its more or less normal position. As he set off back to the hospital he was suddenly overcome by doubts that the case might be more serious than he first thought. Textbooks were rapidly consulted before dashing back to the patient. A baby was being bathed in front of the kitchen fire, but he hardly noticed as he rushed up the stairs to remedy his treatment. He was immediately grasped in gratitude to the patient's ample bosom; his simple binder had to his amazement corrected the alignment of the womb and led to the birth of a healthy baby within minutes of his initial departure.

He then did a locum for a very busy general practitioner, who was taking a belated honeymoon, who naturally assured him (locums were scarce) that there was nothing to worry about – no maternity cases in the offing and no difficult patients. Events soon belied this: in the first twenty-four hours he was called to a pregnant lady who was waterlogged from the crown of her head to the soles of her feet. Her baby was already dead but she was finding it difficult to write '*finis*' to the episode. After two or three unproductive visits he sat on the edge of her bed and told her a few funny stories. She was a big woman with a great sense of humour. Between them they laughed out the baby and all was well. The only problem was that the husband seemed to hold John Henry responsible for the stillbirth.

One night when he was retiring to bed about midnight, the doorbell rang and he was summoned to the Ballygomartin Road to see an old lady who had just returned from an excursion to the Isle of Man. She had been vomiting copiously and was surrounded by her son, two concerned daughters and several grandchildren. My father expressed the opinion that she had merely eaten unwisely on her picnic since she looked reasonably well. However, he had to be seen to earn his five shilling fee, so he took her pulse and happened to take up both wrists. He found the pulse full and of normal rate so he let both wrists fall. Her left arm fell limp and he suddenly realised that he had a patient with a 'stroke' on his hands. His hospital training had never introduced him to the incipience of such a vascular catastrophe. However he said nothing, but taking the son outside he told him that he had not wanted to disturb his sisters or the grandchildren but the truth was much more serious. If he had wished to stay in general practice his fortune was made.

On that admittedly atypical night he was called out a further four times, on each occasion to a serious illness. There was a child (with a saddle-shaped nose – a sign of congenital syphilis) who had measles complicated by bronchopneumonia; a young mother with abdominal pain waiting for admission for an ectopic pregnancy; a man with renal colic; and a baby with meningitis. The latter three patients required hospital admission. He doubted that he saw as much organic disease in the ensuing month as he did on that one night in July. This was his baptism of fire and he felt that his employing GP thoroughly deserved his honeymoon.

There was still a month to go before he was due to take up his hospital appointment at the Royal Victoria Hospital (RVH) which was now confirmed. During the time he was once more to act as locum general practitioner. Having seen the advertisement he went to the lower Falls Road where the practice lay close to the Belfast Model School. He passed the school but saw nothing but a row of small shops and nothing to suggest the residence of a doctor. Yet the street number he had been given by William Fulton, the steward of the Queen's Students' Union, fitted in somewhere in that row of shops. As he paused, a rotund man in a bowler hat and a frock coat, a Dickensian type, enquired if he was Dr Biggart, and on being assured that he was, he introduced himself as 'the Brother' and led him into a shop.

The main window was painted with opaque green paint for more than half its height so that there was privacy from passers-by.

The area, that had once been a shop, had been deprived of its counter and shelves. Instead it was crammed with rows of chairs now occupied by expectant patients. Through the back door of the shop there was a room in which confectionery and tobacco had once been stored and where the shop assistant had boiled her kettle for her cup of tea whilst awaiting the bell that announced the end of school and the imminent inrush of avid little customers. A desk littered with rows of medicine bottles had now replaced all this and behind the desk sat the doctor, a man of nearly seventy, who was wearing a formal morning coat, growing green with age, and with baggy striped trousers a formidable Edwardian member of the profession. John Henry stood in front of him as he was introduced to each row of bottles – one for children suffering from constipation or diarrhoea, one for indigestion, one for coughs or colds, and a most innocuous but highly coloured general tonic. My father was shepherded to a chair in the corner while the old GP proceeded to demonstrate how the practice was run. A thump on the communicating door heralded the arrival of a patient armed with some forms. The GP applied his signature to one side of the document before with a flick of his pencil turning the pro-forma over and again adding his signature. Half a crown was placed on the table – again a flick of the pencil and the coin careered into a metal box nailed to the further side of the desk. Never did the doctor contact the patient, paper or money. When the box became embarrassingly full, the 'Brother' entered, unhinged it, and took it to the kitchen quarters. There he boiled its contents in a saucepan.

My father was greatly intrigued by all this. His studies in anatomy, physiology, pathology and public health had ill-prepared him for practice such as this. As the surgery came to an end, about seven o'clock, he asked this doyen of the profession the whys and wherefores of his method of practice. The reply was interesting. In the early years of the century he had been involved in a typhus epidemic and had ever since had a phobia about contracting the disease. He had not the least idea about its pathology or the role of the louse in its spread, but somehow he knew that personal contact was potentially dangerous, and so in his practice he avoided it with his patients and their belongings. Later my father was to understand his attitude better whilst reading a report in a previous copy of the *Lancet*, written about 1912. It concerned a death in Donegal when the undertaker had refused to come to the home and a doctor and district nurse had had to dig a grave in the back garden and there bury the typhus victim without any benefit of clergy.

Next morning John Henry took over. All he had to do was sign certificates – certificates for ex-servicemen, for tuberculous patients, and for all forms of chronic incapacity. He never had to examine a patient and the suggestion that this was necessary was vehemently resisted. Yet towards the middle of the month, the 'Brother', who was in effect a retired brewer and who was the probable dispenser of the rows of medicaments, suggested that he should take him round the homes of some of the patients. The general purpose of the trip seemed to be to ascertain if the patients for whom my father had signed certificates were still alive and had not emigrated. So eventually, when the practice car arrived at the door, he found himself seated high up on the back seat of a 1912 Ford driven by 'Brother'. Once on the road 'Brother' told him that the car was not insured and indeed not even insurable. Last time out a gust of wind had caused it to overturn. However there was no breeze, and as they passed St Peter's Chapel and my father failed to doff his hat or cross himself, 'Brother' remarked 'I see you're not one of us then.'

Still they visited home after home and for the first time in his life my father saw the conditions in which the people of the lower Falls Road existed – kitchens packed with children whose only chairs were up-turned fruit crates; families of seven or eight head-to-toe in one bed. One patient, unemployed, spent every afternoon in the cinema to escape the harsh realities of life, and on coming home he went to bed – there was nowhere else to go and nothing else to do. Within the requisite few months another small area of the bed would have to be found for the latest arrival. What was a young inexperienced doctor to say? What was he to advise? Possibly the escapism of the cinema or the warm response of his wife prevented or postponed the development of anarchy.

A year later the old doctor broke his wrist and John Henry was again approached. By this time he was an assistant in the Queen's University department of pathology, but by getting the 'Brother' to make the practice hours more suitable, i.e. 9–10 a.m. and 6–7 p.m., he succeeded in earning two incomes. The old doctor, however, came up against it when the Health System – the 'Panel' – reached Northern Ireland in 1931. Never had he had to visit a patient. It was an entirely paper practice, so when a knocking on the door came in 1931 at the unearthly hour of 2 a.m. he stuck his head out the window to listen to the plea of a young husband on behalf of his wife.

He hobbled over to his trousers lying on a chair, fumbled in the pockets, threw the man a ten-shilling note with the advice to go and get a doctor.

Such experiences convinced my father that general practice, which he had idealised as a boy and was the basis of his attraction into medicine, was not for him. Of course he realised that this was by no means a typical general practice but it was a shock that such a practice could exist, and that the old doctor could be so beloved by his patients, as he undoubtedly was.

After his two months of general practice John Henry took up the House Officer's post to which he had been appointed at the RVH. His first attachment was in Wards 15 and 16 under Mr (subsequently Sir) Samuel T. Irwin, but 'Pa' Kirk was the senior surgeon and laid claim to his services. So for the next six months he was 'Pa's house surgeon. As a student my father had been his pupil so he remembered something of his whims and fancies. They 'scrubbed up' wearing unsterilised gloves. Gloves as a result certainly lasted longer than in other wards but my father retained doubts about this practice whilst eventually coming to respect the antibacterial resistance of the peritoneal cavity.

Those were the days when the chiefs were chiefs and were seen to be so. John Henry had to meet 'Pa's car'– an obsolescent coupé – at the front door and accompany 'Pa' to the ward carrying his briefcase. Coffee-time could be prolonged but more often than not the discussion was philosophical rather than medical. He gave John Henry a book by a Jesuit priest to improve his knowledge of prayer. Unfortunately, he had a bad habit of sending in patients at all hours which had the potential to wreck John Henry's love life since tickets for the Opera House, say, or the Hippodrome, could become suddenly useless as a case of perforated duodenal ulcer or acute appendicitis was admitted during dinnertime. Cancellation was one thing; explanation to his future wife patiently waiting for him in the foyer was another. One such evening a patient was admitted about 6 p.m. John Henry hastened to the ward, wrote up the case, arranged an anaesthetist, had the patient prepared for operation, skipped his dinner and stood waiting for the great man. Seven o'clock passed; seven-thirty came and went and by eight he said to the ward sister that he wished 'Pa' would hurry up and come. He heard a voice behind him saying – 'Pa is here' and turning round he discovered that he was.

John Henry had obviously found time amidst all his studies to keep life in balance and do some serious courting. By this time his family had moved from the country to Belfast and were living at 103, The Mount, at

The Biggart family on holiday in Brae.
Front: John Henry, Moira, his father and mother. Rear: Hugh and Florence (1929)

Mountpottinger in East Belfast. On Sunday he attended Ballymacarett Presbyterian Church, where a lovely girl singing in the choir caught his eye. Entranced by her winsome smile and slim figure he went out of his way to find out her name (Isobel Gibson) and sought to get better acquainted. He could not join the choir because he was completely tone deaf and sang off key. It may, therefore, have been for this reason that he joined her as a Sunday school teacher at the church. At any rate by fair means or foul he was successful in his courtship and they soon fell headlong in love. I suppose my mother-to-be considered him relatively handsome and potentially a good catch as a clever medical student. She lived conveniently close to The Mount, at 27, Upper Frank Street just off the Woodstock Road. Her father, David Henry Gibson was employed by the Royal Insurance Company and rose to become its Chief Inspector. Her mother, Jane (née Bowden) was the daughter of a Master Mariner, James Bowden, and his wife, Annie. Interestingly, Jane and her twin brother, James, were born in October/November 1885 in the middle of the Indian Ocean aboard their father's ship, HMS *Elinor*. The twins were registered in Bombay three weeks later when the ship docked. Unfortunately, the male twin, James, succumbed after a few weeks. My mother, Isobel, was the youngest of three children. Her sister, Annie, who was eight years her senior, became a highly regarded teacher in Mountpottinger School, before marrying a solicitor, Henry McKee, and emigrating to Canada. Annie had a turbulent marriage before divorcing and returning to Ulster for the rest of her life. My mother's brother, Harry, never married. He became an agent, selling hospital equipment to local hospitals. He was the author of several successful kitchen comedies performed in the Ulster Group Theatre in the 1940's and 1950's. Amongst his successes were *The Square Peg*, *Uncle Dan* and *Bannister's Café*. In September, 1950 a new young actor gave an impressive performance. His name was William Millar, later to become famous on stage and screen as Stephen Boyd.

My mother's father, David Henry Gibson, had died in 1918 when she was only thirteen and she had been then forced through financial stringency to leave Methodist College and enter the Royal Insurance Company as a typist. She and her brother and sister were then raised by their widowed mother, Jane. Eventually their mother bought a new house and the family moved to 30 Green Road, Knock. John Henry and Isobel became engaged shortly after his graduation in 1928.

Remarkably, in addition to his love life, John Henry found time to participate in amateur dramatics. He was a member of the now defunct National Drama League and wrote at least two plays: one was a kitchen comedy about a widowed woman in a County Down village and entitled *The End of the Year* presumably based on his knowledge of Ballygowan life; while the other was a tragedy entitled *My Son* set in a North Antrim fisherman's cottage. It is gratifying that this was written eight years before my own arrival into the world.

John Henry dressed for his part in
Playboy of the Western World (1928)

Returning to the hospital environment, 'Pa' Kirk was a great believer in nursing sisters trained in the great London hospitals, and an admirer of surgeons of originality, such as Abernethy and Lister. The common practice, the current fashions were not for him. There were so many things in which he demanded the expression of his originality – his own way of making and applying splints, of sterilising cat-gut, of treating breast cancer, of trying to avoid wound infection. John Henry felt however that he was less than strict at assessing critically his own results.

The senior physician was Dr John Morrow. When a young man he had accompanied Lord Pirrie, chairman of the Hospital Board and of ship-building fame, on a cruise. Soon after his return he was appointed (in 1903) to the Assistant Staff and (in 1918) to the full (Honorary) Attending Staff and through weight of years had by this time become the senior physician. Originally he had intended to be a surgeon but he had developed an infection of the palm of his left hand which resulted in a stiff middle finger. In the discussion of a problem he had the habit of massaging this finger, and those around him swiftly learned that this heralded an imminent explosion. There was one occasion at the beginning of the university term when one of the new students was standing in the alcove at the students' entrance to the main hospital corridor, and as he waited he smoked his pipe. Round the corner came Johnny, noticed the pipe, and informed the student, who was completely unaware of his identity, that smoking in the corridor was prohibited. Johnny walked away but after a few yards he returned to the student, Hugh Graham – 'I hope you don't mind what I said to you'. The student dutifully replied that he did not mind in the least. But Johnny had started to massage his finger and his reply was – 'you don't mind? Well, by ———, I'll make you!' That student subsequently gave up medical studies and being endowed with a beautiful baritone voice became a member of the D'Oyly-Carte Opera Company.

So it was with some trepidation that John Henry moved towards 1 and 2 to act as Johnny's house physician. My father was a pipe-smoker, as 'Pa' Kirk had been, but obviously coffee-time was to be different in future. He was taken round the ward by his predecessor and introduced to the patients and their ailments. Later that morning Johnny came to find out what topic he could teach on the following day. My father showed him a boy of twenty who was reported to have developed neuritis in his legs after an attack of influenza, and so next morning Johnny gave the clinical class an exposition on post-influenzal polyneuritis. Next day, having settled in, John Henry examined the patient in more detail. He discovered that the patient had bilateral pes cavus and so had no difficulty in recognising Friedreich's Ataxia. So two days later he introduced him with this diagnosis to Johnny, who obediently and without the slightest sign of recognition taught upon him once more.

There was a tradition in the ward that Johnny always liked to score off his house physician – to find some fault in the clinical history, or in the physical

House Officers RVH. John Henry is standing at extreme left of group (1929)

examination, or an omitted laboratory test. It was therefore of advantage for his houseman to leave some obvious gap in the patient's record, as it gave Johnny such obvious pleasure to highlight the deficiency. Apparently this practice originated when Dr R. Sydney Allison had been his house physician. He was most competent, wrote up progress notes on his patients each and every day, had all the requisite tests performed, and poor old Johnny had no excuse to show his authority as chief. Yet on one occasion Allison slipped up. It was a case of haematuria and in his progress notes he had written that the patient had 'vomited once or twice yesterday'. Johnny read the note, rubbed his finger and turning to Allison exclaimed 'now, Dr Allison, did he vomit once or did he vomit twice? For heaven's sake let us have some investigation in this ward.'

The chief was also physician to Harland and Wolff shipyard – a relic of his early association with Lord Pirrie, the chairman. A company employee was admitted to the ward and was examined by John Henry. He had reputedly fallen down a ladder and was having pain in his genital region. After examination my father was satisfied that the real complaint was gonorrhoea. The sister in charge of the ward, however, was a most charming woman, small and prim and stemming from the Victorian era. He felt that she would have delighted Florence Nightingale, but young and inexperienced as he was, he felt that she would be shocked if she were to learn that she was housing such a patient in her ward. He therefore wrote up the case history in Latin – 'ante injuriam, habet coitum' etc. Next morning Johnny arrived with all his retinue, read all the case notes, gave thanks to God that he had a scholarly houseman and approached the patient. Whereupon the following dialogue developed:

> Andy – 'What is the matter with me, doctor?'
> Johnny – 'Andy, do you really want to know?'
> Andy – 'Yes, doctor'
> Johnny – 'Well, Andy, you have got the clap, the C.L.A.P!'

At this both the patient and the demure little sister collapsed.

The modern house officers justifiably complain of their workload but the house officers in those early days worked at least as hard. Each had fifty beds under his or her care, with one resident student pupil to help. It also fell to them to carry out certain tasks in the Medical Outpatients' Department. One unit did all the test meals – so popular at that time in the investigation of gastric disorders; another did all the simple blood tests. There were few of the intermediate grades of medical staff that are prevalent today. There was, of course, the benefit of being continuously in close contact with the consultants, who in spite of their idiosyncrasies taught their juniors to be good bedside observers and much besides of the art of medicine.

Rarely did John Henry go to bed before one or two in the morning. Life, however, was good. There were the forbidden suppers with the night nurses in the ward kitchens about midnight, made all the more savoury because of the danger of being caught by the Night Superintendant, Sister Dynes. Although apparently austere, she had a great deal of common sense, and she somehow managed to keep away from the ward at critical moments. It was the recognised duty of every entrant to the ward, except the Night Superintendant, to give an explosive cough on entry, and when the door banged and there was no such warning, it was amazing what could happen in the ward kitchen in a matter of seconds. Escape was aided by the fact that the kitchen had two diametrically placed exits.

Sister Dynes had held the position since the hospital had opened its doors on its new site in 1903. She was a pious Catholic, austere, sober, steadfast and demure. A woman of great character – she earned the respect of all the housemen. John Henry remembered an instance on his last night at residence. He claims to have been the only completely sober houseman that night and did the night rounds from Wards 1 and 2 to Wards 19 and 20. Somewhere along the corridor he met her, took her in his arms and kissed her. It was as if he had defiled the *Pieta* of Michelangelo. Years later when he returned as Professor of Pathology he met her in that very same spot in the corridor and he did not think that the twinkle in her eye was the product of his own fancy.

In those days there was intense competition to gain senior appointments in the teaching hospitals. The number of posts was much smaller than today. Each was entirely a voluntary office, not required by law or medical authorities, and the majority of graduates went straight into general practice. However, residency was not all work. John Henry and his friends enjoyed themselves even though they were fairly consistently confined to the hospital precincts. Their salary of a resident house officer was only £40 per annum, but they accepted this without grumbling. They were at last doing what they had set out to do. With free residence, free food, and a pound to spend on their one evening a week when off duty, life was considered very pleasant.

There was a great sense of professionalism, and as they carried their chiefs' briefcases from their cars many of them looked forward to a day of similar affluence and influence.

For his final three months John Henry was appointed to the Casualty Department – a busy and responsible post sometimes made more onerous by having to ensure the presence of resident pupils at their dressing stations at their appropriate times. Busy as every day was, the real climax was reached on Friday and Saturday nights when the department was overrun by party revellers overloaded with drink. One female patient who he had adjudged to be unconscious removed a large hatpin and inserted it with great force in his chest. Luckily she struck a rib, for she was full of 'red biddy' and totally out of touch with her actions. There was then, as we have come to know in the not too distant past, the weekend riot, and there was much experience to be gained in traumatic surgery.

It was during this period (1928–36) that the RAC International Tourist Trophy races were held on the Ards circuit. The race started at Quarry Corner, Dundonald and continued to Newtownards, then Comber, and back to Dundonald, for a total of thirty laps of the thirteen and a half mile circuit. John Henry was quietly listening to the description of the race on his wireless when suddenly chaos broke out in Casualty. At the entrance, the Casualty Sister had already a patient on the trolley and was wheeling him hither and thither, not knowing whether to send him to the ward or the mortuary. Outside the door were two breakdown lorries with their crane around which lay some fourteen men who had been involved in a pile-up on the course. Bones stuck through their denims. Many of the non-resident staff were at the racecourse. Gradually the bodies were disentangled. The Professor of Surgery suddenly arrived direct from the race circuit's grandstand, and from 4 p.m. to 4 a.m. strove to repair the damage. Visitors to the hospital became, almost willy-nilly, blood donors. The housemen typed the blood as best they could, assisted at the suturing of ruptured bladders, at repairing compound fractures, or shattered chests. Incredible as it might seem, not one single patient was lost.

As his year came to its end, John Henry began to consider his future career. Professor Walmsley invited him to be his assistant in anatomy and Professor Milroy did likewise in physiology, but the man who had impressed him most was Professor Symmers in pathology. So one afternoon he went to visit him. It was the afternoon of Symmer's final lecture since he was due to retire, but he kindly appointed my father so that his successor had no say in the matter.

The new chief in pathology was Professor Murray Drennan, originally from Edinburgh, but homing back from Otago, New Zealand, where he had held the chair from 1914 to 1929. It was to Drennan that my father attributed the revitalisation of the pathology services in Belfast setting them on the staircase of pathological science. He considered him a charming and always considerate chief, somewhat shyly encouraging, but at the same time expecting results. One day, when Drennan had influenza, John Henry was called on and gave his first lecture; it was on meningitis and he was later shattered to find that this topic featured as a question on the students' examination paper. Like all beginners he had attempted to be all-embracing in his exposition and had demonstrated, amidst a wealth of other material, the one and only case of anthrax meningitis that the department had ever seen. Needless to say the one type of meningitis that no student failed to mention in the exam was that caused by anthrax, whilst the common types were more cursorily treated. It was a good lesson for a beginner, but one which, as a teacher, he never forgot in his later academic career.

His two years as assistant in the Pathology Department passed quickly. Because of the comparatively poor funding of the University – the University Grants Committee had been omitted as a result of the 1920 Government of Ireland Act – technicians were few and far between, but those present were kindly and competent and remained his good friends throughout his working life. Lorrain Smith, when he was appointed the first Professor of Pathology in Belfast in 1901, had stolen one of them from Edinburgh, Robert McGregor Stevens ('Stevie' to all and sundry). From him John Henry learned the current techniques, for in order to see any results from his research he had to carry out his own technical procedures. So he found that the average day extended from 9 a.m. until midnight. His day embraced post-mortems, teaching, cutting surgical specimens, and staining sections for microscopic examination. It was often 1 a.m. before he reached home by walking the two miles or so to Mountpottinger. There he often found that his considerate mother had left him a plate of cold ham, a potato or two in the pot, plenty of butter and possibly a raw onion. The hard work paid off and in 1931 he was awarded the degree of M.D. (with Gold Medal) by Queen's for his thesis into the function of the white blood cell known as 'the eosinophil'.

Towards the end of John Henry's second year, Professor Drennan suggested that he apply for the prestigious Commonwealth (now Harkness) Fellowship. Since its inception only two Queen's staff members had received this award – one in Biochemistry and one in Engineering. So without much hope, my father filled in the requisite forms and duly appeared in London for the interview, feeling every bit 'the wee country lad from the back of beyond'. The other contenders including the future Lord Crowther-Hunt and Lord Penny, a British poet, leaders in physics and chemistry, litterateurs, economists and one other medical from a London hospital. However, as they waited apprehensively, the other medical candidate seemed to my father to be pompous and somewhat aggressive. This raised John Henry's hackles so that his circulating adrenaline levels were still high as he was called for interview. Whether because of this or not, he felt that he had acquitted himself reasonably well but was nevertheless astounded when a few days later he was notified that he had been awarded a Fellowship to Johns Hopkins Medical School in Baltimore. America now beckoned.

Chapter 6

United States of America

The then Prince of Wales was Patron of the Commonwealth Fund and received the successful applicants at St James' Palace. As John Henry stepped backwards following his introduction to the Prince, to his great embarrassment he pirouetted on the Lord Chancellor's toes. At the subsequent dinner he had the pleasure of meeting the writer, Eric Linklater, who had just returned from his Fellowship years (1920–30). He found that Linklater had a longer and more esoteric horde of good stories than himself, so from then on he bought every one of his publications.

On the night prior to departure from Belfast he said all his emotional good-byes to his family and his tearful fiancée. He gave expression to his emotional side by presenting her with a sonnet poem that he had written for the occasion:

LOVE IN ABSENCE

Remember me when I am gone away
Gone far away unto another place
Where I no more can look into your face
Smiling in welcome, entreating you to stay.
Remember me when I can no longer say
Sweet words of joy and love to you or trace
The marks of ever-present care upon your face,
Or reason how to smooth them all away.
Fair days will come, delay awhile, and go.
Dark nights will follow, urging us to sleep.
With night sweet visions come, our thoughts will flow
Back to each other, quickening us to keep
Remembrance of our love, which thus will grow
And spring up in our hearts, more strong, more deep.

It seems unlikely that this offering would have helped to quell my future mother's floods of tears, but it was something for her to treasure and keep under her pillow in her loneliness over the next two years.

On the next evening, the night of departure, he was dined in the home of Lord Justice Best. Eric Lindsay, the astronomer and future Head of the Armagh Observatory, who was also sailing, was a fellow-guest. Dinner progressed and the marble clock sounded the hour for their departure. The clock, however, was slow and as they reached the ship preparations to remove the gangway were already under way. Lindsay had yet to buy his ticket and John Henry's trunk was still in the left-luggage office. He appealed to the sailor in charge of the gangway to delay the departure even for a minute. 'Mister, I can't hold the bloody boat,' was the reply, but somehow or other they scrambled on board.

From Liverpool they embarked on the RMS *Britannic*. There were sixteen Fellows, only one of whom was female. The British bard amidst them fell romantically in love with the lady and after dinner the other ten or twelve took delight in forming an impenetrable wall around her, thus denying the poet access to her. However, it all proved to be in vain for she later married him.

The voyage was pleasant, incorporating a mixture of lazing in the sun, playing deck tennis and intellectually stimulating conversation amongst a very assorted group of academics. They spent an enjoyable Sunday in Boston Harbour before proceeding to New York. The Fellows were shepherded to the Custom's shed according to their names, but John Henry had had the foresight to realise that there might be a considerable number of 'B's so he had labelled his entire luggage with the letter 'Z'. Not surprisingly he found himself the only traveller in that particular bay.

After a few days in the Pennsylvania Hotel, entertained lavishly by the millionaire son of the founder of the Fellowships, they were dispatched to their various universities not to meet again until some years later at the annual dinner in London.

On being introduced into his new pathology laboratory environment at Johns Hopkins, John Henry was thrilled on being appointed Professor W.G. McCallum's personal assistant. He worked also with the famous Arnold Rice Rich, and got to know that most legendary pathologist – William H. 'Popsy' Welch, one of the 'Big Four' who had launched and steered the Johns Hopkins Medical School on its influential course towards world wide fame for its original medical research and therapy (the other three were William Osler as physician, William S. Halsted as surgeon and Howard A. Kelly as gynaecologist), and the subjects of the famous group portrait *The Four Doctors* by John Singer Sargent. For some reason or other 'Popsy' Welch, then nearing eighty years, took a strong liking for my father. Though retired from pathology and at this time foundation professor of the history of medicine at Johns Hopkins, he was still well informed about the subject, but when John Henry dined with him in the Maryland Club the

W.G. McCallum, Professor of Pathology, Johns Hopkins (1931)

subjects discussed into the early hours of the morning tended to be matters of philosophy, medical history, or classical mythology. McCallum also showed his pictures of Bali before the earthquake and talked of many things. In their company my father met many men of international renown and was stimulated not only in his chosen subject but also in many of the broader aspects of life. 'Popsy' could still give an excellent lecture without a note. McCallum was one of the most intellectually honest of men, from whom John Henry learned that it was a virtue to admit ignorance and so avoid useless hypotheses.

Rich too was a great stimulus. He had an excellent analytical mind with an interest in the esoteric in pathology. The departmental Journal Club met in his home each Monday evening at seven o'clock. For an hour they were entertained to a musical quartet, in which Rich played the violin and his wife the piano. Sometimes the inevitable analysis of the medical papers, which had been read during the week, was postponed by the obstreperous behaviour of their baby daughter, Adrienne, who was later to become one of the foremost poets and radical feminist critics in America. After the musical interlude they settled down to their Journal Club activities until, about eleven o'clock, supper was brought in. For another hour or so the group then indulged in some sort of philosophic argument. On one occasion they sought to obtain a definition as between Science and Art, and though John Henry thought he had solved the problem by stating that Science was the transference of matter into the mind, and Art the transference of mind into matter, Rich was not satisfied and continued his endless search for the ultimate definition.

Every morning the day started with a lecture to the medical students, and after the professor had given a few introductory lectures, the remainder was delegated to the other members of staff including John Henry, who had to take his share. He found the presence of the other staff members in the front row of the lecture theatre a stimulus to his reading about his allotted topic in depth, for most of them were senior to him. The American students were older than their British counterparts since they were mainly already graduates of a College or even University, and they thus made more use of current journals than textbooks. Their respect was gained, not by one's position in the department, but by demonstrating a questioning attitude to the established medical theory.

My father had intended to continue his research studies on the white blood cell known as the eosinophil, but upon consultation with Professor McCallum it was decided to devote the two years of the Fellowship to research on 'Prostatic Hypertrophy' as this was considered one of the most important problems of the moment. Accordingly the studies on eosinophilia were brought to a conclusion and in due course presented in thesis form for the degree of Doctor of Medicine at Queen's University, Belfast, which was awarded (with Gold Medal) in 1931. His other duties included the performance of many autopsies from which he laid a foundation stone of knowledge that he retained and put to great use in later years. He was fascinated by the American cult of death. It was common to have the deceased embalmed and the facial mask of death obscured by the injection of formalin and paraffin wax to eliminate the wrinkles. The deathly pallor of the cheeks was made more roseate even than in life by the use of cosmetics before the body was displayed to friends and relatives in the best suit or dress. Morticians, funeral parlours and cemeteries all participated in the cult. Reputable newspapers carried advertisements for 'sunny sites' in burial grounds, promised 'female embalmers for female patients' and carried pictures of the city's outstanding embalmers. The wakes of Ireland paled beside the plush velvets of the funeral parlours. It is interesting that this cult has persisted and even grown since that time and it is now possible, if desired, to display one's deceased and reconstituted relative in a raised coffin behind a glass window as the busy mourners drive past and nod their respects.

The very expert hospital mortician was a Bavarian. Prohibition was still the order of the day though Maryland had never enacted the Volstead Act of 1919 and supposedly applied until 1933, and it was only when the Federal Police became interested that alcohol would temporarily disappear. As it was, the mortician was a bootlegger, and when performing an autopsy it was only necessary to hint that the liquor store was running low and that evening the matter was mysteriously corrected. On one such occasion, when John Henry came out to his car, he found a policeman leaning on the edge of his open car window through which could be seen a gallon of whiskey sitting on the passenger seat. The policeman reprimanded him for leaving his car window open but ignored the illegal bottle of spirits. In fact in the laboratory, and with the help of the technicians, he distilled his own gin; the only problem was to ensure that the absolute alcohol had been distilled from a glass and not a copper retort.

In a restaurant in Franklin Street in downtown Baltimore a waitress once spilled a jug of cream down his suit. He made no fuss, and as a result found that for the next two years he was supplied with two cream jugs for his coffee – one filled with cream, the other with a liqueur. Indeed, if the Federal Police were not there, it was possible to watch the barrels of beer being unloaded and deposited in their cellars. It was reminiscent of how the problems of food rationing were avoided in Northern Ireland during the two world wars. Yet though he had so much to interest him both in the academic sphere and in the contrast between bustling American life and the relatively plodding pace in Northern Ireland, he often felt homesick and missed his family

Isobel in 1932 waiting for
return of her fiancé from USA

and the comforting arms of his fiancée. Indeed he was once more stimulated to write to her in verse:

TO ADMIRANDA

It's golden like the setting sun
My darling's eyes are bright and blue
Her lips are cherry red
And the snowdrop with its crown of white
Envies her pale forehead.
And when she smiles the dimples play
Upon her pretty cheeks
And her little mouth now tempts, entices –
Now blushes fire her cheeks.
And her hair hangs most bewitchingly
In clusters round her head
When the lightsome day is sped.

One lunchtime, in nostalgic mood, he was sheltering in the doorway when two burly sailors passed, and he heard one of them utter an oath he had only heard in Belfast. So in spite of the rain he dashed out and put the 'spake' on them and greeted them like long lost brothers. He had heard correctly, they were in fact from Belfast, and in a few weeks time one of them returned to tell him that their sugar boat from Cuba had false bunkers and that they were able to supply any type of beverage that the Department might require. So although John Henry considered himself a law-abiding person, the department, throughout its six floors, sported cases of champagne, brandy, scotch, bacardi and sherry following the introduction of his sailor compatriot to the departmental staff.

About two months after his arrival John Henry stepped into the street to be greeted by a Queen's graduate, Dr Alec Martin, a local psychiatrist, who had been told of his Fellowship at Johns Hopkins by his old friend, Dicky Hunter in Belfast. Suddenly he found himself introduced into the social whirl of Scottish and Ulster life. Many of the friends that he met at that time were still his friends some forty years later. Amongst them was Louis Erskine, treasurer of a vast oil complex, who occasionally wrote cheques for over $1,000,000. John Henry had the uncomfortable experience of sitting with him in 1932 as the radio recited one stock failure after another and Erskine heard that the investments that he had made for the future of his son were often now worthless. Erskine was a charming man, but socially shy, and though brought up in a very Presbyterian atmosphere in Holywood, County Down, found it necessary to have a few drinks before any social occasion. So in 'Prohibition' America his study was ringed with cider jars filled with rye whiskey or gin. This was not uncommon in those days. My father recalled a Senator, who was a very strong advocate of Prohibition, holding a reception at which every form of alcoholic beverage was produced. Being young and brash John Henry probed his rationale on this. He was informed that while it was permissible at his social level it would be quite wrong for his underlings. Whether right or wrong this was a fairly common attitude to the problem. When eventually Prohibition was abolished and replaced by 3% beer, it was still possible to go to the illegal restaurants where spirits, wine, and European beer were being served. A Carlsberg or Tuborg was definitely preferable to the local brew.

John Henry had an apartment in the Homewood residences owned by the University. The warden was an amalgam of psychiatrist and historian, a descendant of a professor of chemistry at Harvard who had once wiped out a debt he owed to the professor of anatomy by murdering him. He then attempted to get rid of the evidence by incinerating the body in his laboratory stove. Even Oliver Wendell Holmes was held in suspicion for a time.

Map tracing John Henry's vacation trip across USA (1932)

John Henry in Texas (1932)

However, bones do not disappear easily and false teeth and gold fillings have a habit of establishing identity. The warden, however, was quite proud of his ancestry. In 1912 he had fallen in love with an Austrian duchess and when the First World War broke out had joined the Austrian army in order to take what care he could of her son. His *pièce de résistance* was a dramatic account of his ancestor's exploits.

One of the great assets of the Commonwealth Fellowship was that it supplied additional funds to enable the Fellows to travel throughout the States during their summer vacation. Steele was the only other Commonwealth Fellow at Hopkins. So at the end of the year he and John Henry pooled their resources, bought the first Ford V8 to enter Maryland, and started off on a holiday of a lifetime. Travelling south through Virginia, Tennessee and Alabama they stayed at motels and YMCAs though dining at the best hotels. Many of them were remarkably cheap, as the main holiday season had not yet begun. They spent a few days at New Orleans taking photographs and drinking the dense southern coffee. Then across Texas, New Mexico and Arizona as they drove towards the West. On the way they explored every National Park – the Carlsbad Caverns and the country of Billy the Kid, Mesa, the Painted Desert, the South rim of the Grand Canyon, Bryce and Zion. From New Orleans onwards they used only their camp beds. They tended to drive in the evening to the vicinity of a town. There they changed, wrapped themselves in blankets and were eventually awakened by the sun, before motoring into the best hotel in town, where they washed and breakfasted. Sometimes their sleep was rudely interrupted by intruders or, on one morning, by a tribe of children and their schoolmarms, as they hopped about trying to get their trousers on.

Nineteen-thirty-two was the year of the Olympic Games in Los Angeles, and as Steele and my father generally wore khaki shirts and shorts they were often mistaken for competitors making their way towards the coast. By the time they arrived at the El Piso Hotel on the southern rim of the Grand Canyon they had been in the desert for several days. Entering the dining room, already full of the grand dames in their black lace gowns, the headwaiter was so nonplussed that he placed them at the best table in the bay window. Indeed the average American must have had a problem in trying to work out who they were. They were seemingly moneyed, non-American, and obviously very different. In fact the only contribution that they made to the Olympic Games was their attendance at the opening ceremony.

Then on to San Francisco and along the Pacific coast through the magnificent red woods to Canada, the Fraser River valley, to the Yukon and lumber camps, reindeer and grizzly bears. At one of the lumber camps the cook turned out to be one of John Henry's old schoolmates. Throwing their beds out on the snowline of Mount Rainier they were occasionally wakened by reindeer or a bear stealing their peaches. Eventually on a goat track they found their way across the Rockies and came down into a village of Greeks, who produced an excellent meal of tinned foods, tastefully displayed on the whitest of bedspreads. And so to Banff and back to the USA and Yellowstone, Glacier National Park, and the North rim of the Grand Canyon, Monument Valley, and on to Chicago. Between them they had now only two dollars, but

Opening ceremony of Olympic Games in Los Angeles (1932)

they booked into the best hotel and used the money to telegraph the Commonwealth Fund. In the meantime they walked round the Al Capone territory, and returning to the hotel about 10 p.m. my father heard his name, complete with initials, being called to the telephone. Nobody in the world could have known that he was there. Yet when he went to the booth he found that the phone call had already been accepted and he realised that somewhere in the hotel was someone with exactly the same name as himself. Unfortunately he had already left when John Henry surfaced for breakfast the next morning.

The next afternoon at 3 o'clock, once again in funds, they said goodbye to some friends in Fort Wayne, Indiana, and set off for Hopkins some six hundred and fifty miles away. John Henry was scheduled to lecture there at 8 a.m. next morning. So they drove all through the night with frequent stops in coffee bars. As dawn broke they were through the Maryland Mountains and after a quick refreshing bath my father duly appeared on the lecture rostrum at the stated time.

This holiday made an indelible impression on him and even forty years later he could recall many of the incidents and escapades. There was the evening when they crossed the border on foot to El Mexicale – a town existing entirely as the consequence of the Prohibition Act – and there they had dinner enlivened by a couple of whiskies. Unfortunately their waiter decided that after such an evening their counting ability must have been impaired and he multiplied their bill by four. They left him alone in his glory but minus any payment, as they slipped out through a toilet window before hastening back in some trepidation across the border. They had discovered that though their passports were supposed to be valid in every country with the exception of the USSR, Mexico had apparently been omitted, and the USA was much

John Henry hanging out his washing in Los Angeles (1932)

John Henry's Ford V8 in tunnel through giant sequoia tree (1932)

easier to get out of than to enter or re-enter. Fortunately the border guard failed to notice the deficiency. Encouraged by this they crossed the border into Mexico, again from California, and had a somewhat lucky day at the horse races in Agua Caliente.

One of their adventures could have had a fatal outcome. They set off into the desert to find the cliff dwellings at Betatakin only two or three miles from the road where they had parked the car. It was an hour's walk or so they had been told. On their way they encountered canyons of varying shapes and sizes. They clambered up and down and around. They had been assured that the journey was easy and that if they started early they could be back by mid-day, so they had neither compass nor food. They had not, of course, been told of the two Americans who had gone on the same journey a week before and who had not yet found their way back, and so they kept plodding on. Mid-day came and went. The afternoon temperature rose to 110°F. They grew hot and thirsty and their lips and tongue became parched. Then John Henry remembered how his professor of botany, James Small, had scoffed at anyone suffering or dying from thirst in a desert where cacti abounded, and so they uprooted a small barrel cactus and attacked it with their only weapon – a gold pencil – and eventually obtained some of the internal juices. When they had imbibed what they could, they found that their new condition proved worse than the first; not only was it the most astringent fluid that they had ever tasted, but their lips and tongue became immobilised. Not before time they grimly accepted that they were lost and decided to separate, one walking towards the setting sun and the other towards the east. Within a few minutes my father saw in the face of the cliff, the dwellings that they had been trying for so long to find. In the dying sun he managed to take a few photographs before clambering laboriously up the side of the canyon. There in the distance he could just make out his friend, high on the top of a mound, gesticulating wildly. He had found the car. So they returned to the point where they had set out fourteen hours earlier – very relieved and very lucky to have survived. They once more threw out their camp beds, bought tins of grape-fruit juice and chipolatta sausages and swilled down 'gallons' of Coca-Cola. Gradually all the astringency of the cactus juice was washed away and John Henry's equanimity returned as he was once more able to enjoy the pleasure of his beloved pipe. As they lay down on their beds a chorus of coyotes broke the silence, and in the morning they found that the remnants of their evening meal had disappeared.

My father enjoyed his second year at Johns Hopkins even more than the first. Social life had stabilised and he had made many friends. The only catastrophe was the moratorium declared by the banks, which froze his few savings intended for an Easter in Florida. However, a letter from the Chase Bank containing cash beat the moratorium by one day! Financially he had had more than his share of bad luck. In 1931 as he basked in the sunshine of Boston Harbour, England had gone off the gold standard and next day 'the pound in his pocket' had considerably shrunk in value.

His hospital routine had now become established. He carried out much experimental work as to the possible cause of prostate gland enlargement in the elderly, finally establishing a working hypothesis based on endocrine dysfunction. His theory was supported by Professor McCallum and later by Professor Murray Drennan in Edinburgh, but he was unable to continue with the project as it would have taken several more years to develop further. He therefore decided to study the endocrine functions of the pituitary gland at the base of the brain and the thyroid gland in the neck: work which led to the publication of papers on the role of the anterior pituitary gland and on experimental exophthalmic goitre.

At the medical school there was an abundance of seminars. Teaching duties were over by lunchtime, leaving the afternoon for the completion of his routine work and his research pursuits. One night per week he returned to the laboratory where, before the critical eyes of Professor McCallum and Dr Rich, the junior pathologists sought to demonstrate that they really understood the disease process. The weekly conferences with Drs Hamman and Rich were marvels of clinical deduction, often stretching the pathologist to the limit in endeavouring to define the scientific problems posed by the clinical exposition. There was an atmosphere of deep involvement in the basic problems of disease. Medical meetings were still graced by 'Popsy' Welch and Howard Kelly (two of the original four founders of the medical school), Lewis Weed in anatomy, John J. Abel in pharmacology, Walter Dandy in neuro-surgery, Hugh Young in urology, and a host of others who shone only slightly less brightly than these luminaries. It was a heady atmosphere for a young man.

Years later, in 1964, when John Henry returned to the USA to look at its systems of medical education, he was to find that pathology had undergone a complete reversal of direction. The study of the autopsy and the stimulus which such study gave to research into human disease, was out of favour. Sound experimental pathology based on such studies had given place in many laboratories to experiment for the sake of experiment. Often he suspected that the availability of a new technical advance in apparatus was being credited with more importance than original ideas. The young pathologist built or had built some complicated piece of equipment which he often continued to use long after it had made or failed to make its contribution. It was true that one medical school boasted of its eight electron microscopes reserved for students. It was true that seven were currently out of order, but still their chromium was bright and they made an impressive sight all in a row. Another microscope could produce a logarithmic curve of the DNA content of one thousand cell nuclei. It was true that it was a prototype built to render the diagnosis of cervical smears as non-subjective as possible. It was, however also true that it had failed in its specific purpose, but still each and every smear was subjected to its impersonal stare, and the resultant data duly recorded. Professors of pathology no longer emphasised the value of morbid anatomy as one of their tools, and the association between laboratory and the clinical wards had become more tenuous. Of course, John Henry agreed that there was room for all types of investigation and investigators under the broad umbrella of pathology. He considered his chosen subject of pathology greater than medicine, but he recognised also that a medical school was most stimulated by research into problems that have their origin in the disease processes of humans.

In the early 1930s, however, Hopkins still existed in its halcyon days. There was much sociability. Students respected their teachers for what they did and not for their position in the hierarchy of staff. There was a curious sense of entity. Living as he did on the Homewood residence, the students whom he faced at hospital were often his dinner companions. On one occasion Adolf Meyer, the eminent Professor of Psychiatry, asked his first year class to let him have a curriculum vitae of their sex histories. That evening John Henry heard a knock on his study door after dinner. It was a student asking for his assistance. So for the next half-hour my father furnished the student with a sexual history worthy of Don Juan or Casanova. Throughout that evening one student followed another until by the sixth his imagination finally failed. Although he got no feedback, he felt sure that the sexual histories that he had helped the students to concoct would have brought much satisfaction to Professor Meyer and bolstered his psychiatric theories.

As a Commonwealth Fellow, John Henry was informed that when his Fellowship expired after two years, he would return to the United Kingdom and disseminate the knowledge that he had gained of American academic life. Yet as the second year drew to a close there was inevitably much to worry about. By accepting a Fellowship, he had cut himself adrift from his former junior posts in the career structure in the United Kingdom. Academic posts were at that time few and far between. In April Professor McCallum invited him to stay at Hopkins, so he wrote to the Commonwealth Headquarters and subsequently received approval for an extension for a third year. Before he had committed himself, however, his former chief, Professor Drennan, who had just moved from Belfast to Edinburgh, wrote to offer him a lectureship in neuropathology and so, superficially at least, his problem was solved.

He had always been interested in neurology and the artistry of gold and silver impregnations coating the dendritic extensions on the various types of nerve cells had fascinated him ever since he had entered pathology. He recognised, however, that there were vast gaps in his knowledge. So until he left Hopkins, in between his experimental work on endocrinology, he tried to master the necessary laboratory and experimental techniques and to absorb as much of the requisite literature as he could.

So in July 1933 he hastened back to Belfast and to his fiancée and family. He had enjoyed the United States, and meeting many of the great and cultured men in medicine at John Hopkins, Harvard, Yale and Cleveland. His social life had been happy and full. He had revelled in the adventure of the American way of life and yet he longed to return to the British way of life, for the time 'to stand and stare', for the joy of proceeding at his own individual pace, and for the cosiness of home.

Chapter 7

Pathologist in Edinburgh

On the 1st September 1933 John Henry took up his post in Edinburgh; not only was he lecturer in neuropathology but also pathologist to the Scottish Asylum's Board. Shortly afterwards he was appointed neuropathologist to the Edinburgh Royal Infirmary where he became closely associated with Norman Dott and his neurosurgical team, and with the neurologists Edwin Bramwell and Ritchie Russell which gave him access to the services of a splendid group of laboratory technicians (now called Medical Laboratory Scientific Officers or MLSOs) who could produce the most beautiful gold and silver impregnations with the same ease as the more routine preparations.

Among his duties as pathologist to the Scottish Asylum's Board my father had to travel around the various mental hospitals and stimulate research. It was an interesting experience for which he found himself ill-prepared having had little to do with psychiatrists previously. In Johns Hopkins there had been Adolf Meyer, but in medical school there had been only the slightest of contacts. His best friend in America had been Dr Alec Martin, a fellow graduate from Belfast and a psychiatrist, but he rarely talked about the subject.

The Medical Superintendents were a mixed lot. One of the more jovial had intended to be a surgeon, but an operative infection in his palm had ended that ambition. He had now become an understanding and fatherly figure for over 1,000 patients, and with an excellent herd of cattle on the hospital farm. Another confidently removed the toxins responsible for acute mania by injection of turpentine! Then there was the Superintendent from Donegal, burdened by a deputy who had studied under Adolf Meyer. My father really enjoyed visiting him. Dinner would consist of salmon freshly caught in the famous river that formed the boundary to the asylum grounds, followed up by partridge from his shoot. After dinner they would play bridge with two homicidal doctors, patients in his hospital, and anyone sensitive to

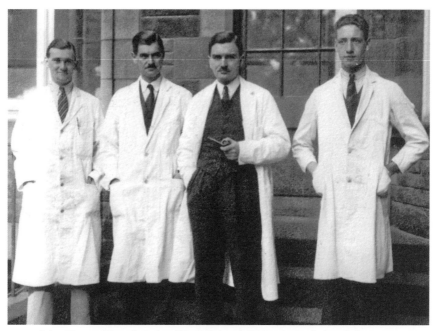

John Henry with technical staff in Edinburgh University Pathology Laboratory.
Bert Russell, soon to move to Belfast, is on extreme left (1936)

atmosphere would think twice before pressing home too vigorously any advantage furnished by his cards. His visits also took him through some of the most beautiful country in Scotland, south to the Border and north to Montrose. At one hospital he asked for the key for the laboratory, and after wrestling successfully with the lock, stiff with disuse, he was swept aside by a cascade of coffins. Yet whether a Superintendent was a farmer, *bon viveur*, or a purveyor of turpentine, or whether he practised his profession on the tenets of Freud, or Jung, or Adler, the annual reports were remarkably uniform with the 'discharged–cured' column showing only a decimal point variation. Most of the Superintendents had an impossible task. Their hospitals were too large, their staff too few, their resources too limited, and apart from one or two honourable exceptions, they were not always of the highest professional calibre. Physical examinations were neither frequent nor detailed, and so in the mortuary John Henry would on occasions come across gross pathology, such as an undiagnosed benign tumour or an old encysted subdural haematoma, as well as a whole wealth of endocrine abnormalities.

In September 1934 my father returned briefly to Belfast to be married, the service being at Knock Presbyterian Church. Bill Basset, a local surgeon, was

Moira Biggart, bridesmaid, Jack McFadzean, groomsman, Theo Bowden, flower girl,
Isobel and Harry, the married couple, Bill Bassett, best man and May McFadzean,
matron of Honour (1934)

best man. The happy couple spent their honeymoon in Torquay, Devon, before taking up rented accommodation in Edinburgh.

Back in Edinburgh Norman Dott and the Edinburgh Royal Infirmary Departments of Neurosurgery and Neurology provided John Henry with numerous cases of interest. George Alexander, soon to become a professor at Bristol, taught him the rudiments of his craft and so enabled him to test a series of autopsy findings experimentally. This enabled him to operate successfully on the brains of dogs, selectively damaging the hypothalamus which resulted in diabetes insipidus. He viewed with some satisfaction the expression on the face of his former professor of surgery in Belfast ('Andy' Fullerton) when, on a visit to Edinburgh, Fullerton while attending an experiment on the hypothalamus, suddenly recognised the face behind the mask as being that of a pathologist! The experimental team gained confidence with the consistency of their results and was soon able to extend the range of its studies. Having in the beginning the objective of learning more about the control of water in the body they soon realised that they were dealing with the essential mechanisms in the preservation of Claude Bernard's 'fixité du milieu intérieur'. Delighted, John Henry envisaged a whole lifetime of

John Henry and Isobel on honeymoon in Torquay, Devon (1934)

interesting problems stretching into his academic future. He was content, and his current research was the basis for a thesis awarded a D.Sc. from Queen's University in 1937 when he returned to Belfast as professor.

Edinburgh at this time appeared to John Henry, a newcomer and one of the few non-Edinburgh graduates on the clinical staff, to be introspective and very much a closed shop. Entertainment was still very formal and an invitation to many of the clinicians' grand houses usually required a white or a black bow tie. In general it appeared to be white for the chiefs, and black for the assistant chiefs.

In his first year in Edinburgh at St Giles House, there was a cross-section of undergraduates and graduates and medicals working usually for their F.R.C.S. from Canada, South Africa and Ireland – undergraduates of various faculties and of varied experience. The doyen of the house was Professor E.B. Jamieson, the famous Edinburgh anatomist whose textbook and other professional publications were widely used and who was credited with remembering every student who had passed through his dissecting room. He looked John Henry paternally in the eye and said '1925, I think' and my father had not the heart to disillusion him – after all he bore a Scottish name, and where else but Edinburgh was a respectable Scot to graduate in medicine? He found it curious that though Edinburgh and Belfast had much the same population structure the attitudes of the citizens to an extent differed. Of course Edinburgh was very old, was the capital of Scotland, and had developed the wisdom and the grace of position, a royal court, and a parliament, etc. Certainly the presence of a senior physician at a dance club with two chorus girls from the 'White Horse Inn' – stolen from their medical student escorts – would have been common knowledge and duly acclaimed by the student body in Belfast. In Edinburgh, however, the only two disconsolate people were apparently the two dispossessed medical students and the physician was duly able to make his round of the wards in his white coat and with reputation unsullied. Such formality and decorum and imperviousness, admirable though they may have been, had repercussions for outsiders such as my father. He found it difficult to penetrate the Edinburgh social circle, which was forever tight knit and introspective. The medical fraternity had gone to the same schools and often had grown up together. There were family dynasties throughout the medical school where son succeeded father and even, as with the anatomists Monro, grandfather. (This experience, paralleled to an extent in Belfast, seemed to make an indelible impression on John Henry as he later strove to introduce national and international figures into the medical school of parochial Ulster, although he failed to apply the same rules for his own family whom he was more than content to keep close to him). As a result many of John Henry's new friends were exiles from Ulster. There was also a constant flow of mainly young surgeons seeking the Diplomas of the Royal College and diplomatically worshipping at the feet of Professor Sir David Wilkie, the highly respected Professor of Surgery at Edinburgh and the President of the Royal College of Surgeons of Edinburgh at that time.

John Henry recalled three such diploma seekers who were not infrequent visitors to St Giles House. On the night preceding their examination, tensions were high and only one accepted his invitation to the Guest Dinner – an annual event attended on that occasion by the Dean of the Medical Faculty. He discovered, however, that the delinquent two had taken themselves off to the Empire Theatre. So with one or two others, and nursing a couple of bottles of Scotch, he hired a taxi and followed them to the theatre. There they had the delinquents paged; but they refused to take the bait. Undaunted, John Henry's little group managed to capture them at the end of the show, and ensured that they slept soundly and completely relaxed before their ordeal of the morrow. Needless to say they were all three successful. In later life, two became heads of their respective departments in Belfast, whilst the third encountered my father twenty years later as the chief surgeon in Penang. On the latter occasion John Henry was more than repaid for his original Edinburgh hospitality.

My father considered that one of the most enjoyable of medical functions was the Edinburgh Pathology Club. Meeting after dinner in the Royal Infirmary the programme might consist of one long or several short papers. It was here that one learnt to concentrate one's material into the minimum of time necessary to convince the audience. Speakers therefore tended to leap from pinnacle to pinnacle leaving the intervening valleys in their 'verdured mystery'. Of course if any of the audience wished to explore these valleys the speaker was always prepared to lead them 'thro' winding paths and verdant mossy ways' and to dally with them over some of the more esoteric trivia. My father always held that many a good piece of research work was lost because its author obscured the wood in describing the trees. One professor, for whom John Henry had prepared serial sections of the middle ear, produced lanternslides of each and every section. His thoroughness was obvious and his paper undoubtedly important in helping his audience to understand the mechanisms of one cause of deafness. However, more than one hundred slides was too much, and when he eventually asked for the light to be switched on he saw that his previously large audience had dwindled to the chairman and secretary of the Society.

At the beginning of his fourth year in Edinburgh, John Henry's small textbook on Neuropathology, *Pathology of the Nervous System,** was published. He found it an amusing interlude in the routine work. It was based on the lectures that he gave to the candidates for the Diploma of Psychological Medicine. When he had arrived at Edinburgh he had found the laboratory strangely deficient in archival material, but he had been exceedingly lucky in obtaining examples of most neurological diseases through the active groups in neurology and neurosurgery. Not knowing how other authors worked, he made a point of writing a chapter each evening after dinner; this ensured that each chapter had a theme which he hoped would be of itself an entity, whilst at the same time a further step up the ladder of the book's thesis. If the chapter

* Biggart J.H.: *Pathology of the Nervous System.* 1936, 1st, 2nd, 3rd eds. E.S. Livingstone, Edinburgh & London. Reprinted 1940, 1949, 1961.

failed to appeal next evening then it was discarded in its entirety and a completely different presentation attempted. During any free time the illustrations were compiled, and the book went to its publishers exactly one month after he had signed the contract.

This little book, so rapidly produced, was to prove a godsend to numerous future medical students and postgraduate students in neurology and psychiatry who were trying to grasp the fundamental rudiments of the diseases of the brain and nervous system. It made no pretence at being an exhaustive study of neuropathological knowledge, but instead set out to describe the known mechanisms of neurological diseases in a lucid and concise manner. It did away with the mysticism and complicated vocabulary that were features of many other text-books of neuropathology of the time, by showing that the brain and nervous system responded in much the same ways to disease as did the other organs of the body. Moreover, it was readable and written in clear, concise prose. Its illustrations were numerous and of excellent quality. It was extremely well reviewed and, at fifteen shillings, was within most students' budgets. The immediate pecuniary return, as was then frequent, was modest – John Henry received £9-10s-6d 'in payment of Royalty due'. Nevertheless, in its first year the book was to become established in most medical school libraries in many countries and, when necessary, was translated into other languages. It was still extremely popular when my sister and I were clinical medical students.

Whilst in Edinburgh John Henry and Isobel lived in rented accommodation at 11 Hartington Gardens and six weeks after the publication of the book their family life was shattered when I made my appearance on 18th November 1936 in a Private Nursing Home, 9 Grosvenor Crescent. The labour was extremely difficult and lasted almost 48 hours, nearly resulting in a Caesarian section. After this horrific experience my mother was adamant that our family was complete. She had no intention of going through such agonies again. She held firmly to this decision for some six years, but then as a symbol of defiance to Hitler, gave birth to my sister, Rosemary in September 1942.

In the spring of 1937 Sir John Cairns came to Edinburgh to offer John Henry an appointment at Oxford, but while he was considering what appeared to be a tempting and exciting opportunity, the Chair of Pathology back home at Queen's fell vacant. His Edinburgh colleagues encouraged him to apply for Belfast in preference to Oxford; but he was filled with self-

John Henry nursing his newly-born son, Denis, in Edinburgh (1936)

doubts. He was only thirty-one and all the Professors of Pathology that he knew were men of maturity – Symmers, Drennan, McCallum, Muir, Shaw Dunn, Matthew Stewart, and so on. There had been occasional young men appointed to Chairs of Physiology and Anatomy, but Professors of Pathology were men rich in experience not only of their subject but also of life itself. Had he not seen other young aspiring pathologists brought down to size when they were making presentations to the Pathological Society of Great Britain and Ireland? Often their English would be criticised, their method of presentation condemned, their reasoning faulted. Woe betides the speaker who read a paper from written notes or exceeded his allotted time. In short he felt, if not incompetent, at least unfledged for the post. However, for his age, he had already acquired an unusual depth of knowledge through his wide experience in research and teaching at Johns Hopkins. It had been Professor McCallum's practice to choose the lectures that he wished to give before allowing his junior staff members to divide the remainder amongst them. John Henry always chose to give the lectures about which he knew least, and as they were attended by most of the staff, no facile exposition could be tolerated. The stored specimens, the files of microscopic slides, and the numerous autopsies that he had performed, had given him the opportunity to acquire a practical knowledge, whilst the Welch library allowed him to keep up-to-date with every relevant topic. In spite of his doubts he was persuaded to apply. Professor Drennan rejected the first draft of his application as being too diffident and he was encouraged to abjure undue modesty and present a forthright shop window of his abilities and qualifications, as a result of which he was short-listed. Among those to be interviewed was a well-established professor in Canada and a fellow Queen's man several years his senior. On the day of the interview he duly presented himself before the Board of Curators. The omens were not favourable: he was suffering from a fever of 103°F and had just heard that his youngest sister was in danger of dying from puerperal sepsis (fortunately she didn't). However, a consoling fact, within his suit pocket was a kindly letter from the Electors at Oxford asking him to submit, if he was unsuccessful, a copy of his Belfast application even though he had already refused their offer of appointment. At the interview the Curators' questions apparently allowed him to discuss his most cherished ideas and he steadily gained confidence due, he later claimed, to fever-induced euphoria. When the candidates were asked to wait, he felt that the Vice-Chancellor was more polite with the other applicants as he graciously thanked them for their attendance; but two days later, as he booked his return to Edinburgh, he met Dr 'Dicky' Hunter, the Secretary of the University, who told him that the Senate had just confirmed his appointment. Bookings were hastily cancelled and a telegram sent to Professor Drennan to explain the reason for his delayed return. The rest of the week was passed in suitable conviviality and family celebration. In fact his mother, once again displaying her unshakable belief in her son's infallibility, had already instigated the gathering of the clan before the interview had even taken place. His cup of joy overflowed when his sister began to show signs of recovery from her childbed fever, in response to administration of the early sulphonamides. Then it was back to Edinburgh to prepare for the challenging job ahead.

Chapter 8

Back to Belfast –
Institute of Pathology

One of the more important books of the Hippocratic Corpus begins by stating – 'to me it seems that there is no beginning, first principle, or starting point of the body, but all things are equally beginning and end, for when a circle is drawn a beginning is not found'. Coming home to John Henry was the completion of that circle. He found that in many ways nothing had changed. He had already visited the new Institute of Pathology on the Royal Victoria Hospital site (opened in 1933) and the new Royal Maternity Hospital on the adjacent, old Asylum site (opened also in 1933) on his return from the United States four years previously. There were new Professors of Biochemistry and Physiology, but Walmsley still held the Chair of Anatomy. Richard, better known as 'Dicky', Hunter no longer taught in Embryology, an irrecoverable loss to the Medical School in my father's eyes. 'Dicky' had always been a friend to the medical students and an adviser *extraordinaire* to members of staff, and it was probably on account of these abilities that he had been enticed into the position of Secretary of the University although he had always advised others who, like himself, loved medicine, to avoid being sucked into a career in administration. Like so many others who have followed this path, paperwork built a barricade rather than a bridge between himself and those whom he loved to teach and serve. John Henry, however, continued to use his former close friendship to his advantage by often calling first thing in the morning, on his way to the hospital, into Dr Hunter's office for a chat on shared problems. In this way he was able to exert influence and ensure that the affairs of the Pathology Department and eventually the Medical Faculty were placed advantageously on the stepladder for their future advancement.

The new Institute of Pathology, owned by the University, was situated adjacent to the Royal Victoria Hospital and linked to it by a bridge. It had only been occupied four years previously, its some 28,000 sq. ft replacing the original pathology facility of 3,000 sq. ft or so on the main Queen's University campus. He returned as a professor and head of department to find that nearly all his colleagues had been his teachers, but this probably worked to his advantage, as he had retained the respect that he had felt for them when he was a medical student.

The siting of the new department adjacent to the hospital resulted in an ever-expanding workload. When appointed in 1937, John Henry inherited a totally insufficient number of support staff for the Institute's growing needs. The University was comparatively poorly funded by government, for when the Treaty that established Northern Ireland as an entity within the United Kingdom was drafted, it had been omitted from the negotiations and the University Grants Committee had in consequence no responsibility to advise on its finance. Indeed it was not until the end of the war that the Vice-Chancellor, Sir David Keir, succeeded in establishing a fruitful liaison between the Northern Ireland Government and the University Grants Committee: only then was it possible to look forward to some improvement and stabilisation of government funding.

Technical and Secretarial Support

When my father arrived, preparation of tissue sections for microscopy was dependent on a very few laboratory technicians. The student teaching laboratory was under the control of a much-loved old character, affectionately known as 'Stevie' (real name, Roderick McDonald Steven). Professor Lorrain Smith, the first Musgrave Professor of Pathology at Queen's (1901–04), had attracted 'Stevie' from Edinburgh when he took up the chair. When John Henry had been a student in the pathology department in 1925 the then professor, William St Clair Symmers, would make a brief appearance and tell the students what they were expected to do before leaving 'Stevie' in control of the practical class where the students had to stain their own sections. He had a solitary assistant, Louis Bell, who had been in the department since 1914. Louis was unfortunately afflicted by a partial paralysis of the left side of his body, having a withered arm and a limp. This handicap prevented him from undertaking the more arduous tasks, but 'Stevie' and Louis were together almost entirely responsible for cutting the tissue sections studied by students over the first half of the century. Louis endeared himself to generations of students by his warm kindliness and interest in their welfare. Remarkably, he could remember most of them by name. He saw them safely into their lectures, often with a smile and a chat, and ensured that the lecture theatre was ready for the professor. At examination time he would often offer a calming word to the jittery student who was about to enter the arena of the *viva*. Throughout their careers both 'Stevie' and Louis continued to serve the student body and medical staff with the same courtesy as they had shown in the early part of the century when the pace of laboratories and life was so much slower. 'Stevie' was to retire in the mid-1940s and died in 1947, but Louis went on to complete a half century in the department, retiring in 1964.

In 1937 the diagnostic laboratory, i.e. the lab concerned with the production of sections of biopsy tissue from surgical patients and autopsy examinations, was in a dire state. A talented young and inexperienced man, Jim Davidson, was the technician in charge and together with another junior somehow managed to process the biopsies for the pathologists to study and issue their diagnostic reports to the wards. The majority of the tissue samples from the post-mortem examinations, however, could only be processed as far as their storage within paraffin wax cubes for later study when staffing levels allowed. The difficulties were compounded when Jim, who had previously joined the Territorial Army to supplement his salary, was mobilised in September 1939 shortly after the outbreak of the Second World War. He later returned from the war to rejoin the technical staff, giving years of loyalty to the department for the rest of his career.

Faced with this unacceptable situation, John Henry remembered the superb technical assistance that he had had whilst working in Edinburgh, and he contacted a young Scottish technician, Robert ('Bert') Russell, who had particularly impressed him. Meanwhile, with the Vice-Chancellor and the hospital management, he had negotiated a salary for a post of Senior Laboratory Assistant. It was by today's standards a very meagre salary, but with the kudos of working as the chief technician for the new professor, it was sufficient to attract Bert Russell and his new Scottish bride, Emily, to Belfast, where they remained thereafter. This was a key appointment. Without someone of Bert's calibre, my father would almost certainly have been unable to transform and develop the quality of the pathology services over the subsequent thirty years. Bert had a puckish sense of humour and always showed a polite deference to his medical colleagues. He was meticulous in every aspect of his work and rejected anything sub-standard, repeating it over

Institute of Pathology, key members of his laboratory staff. (From the left) David Mehaffey,
Jim Davidson, Bert Russell, Cecil Bennet and Jack Reid (*c.* 1964)

and over again until he considered it perfect. The high standards that he set
for himself he demanded of his other technicians to the benefit and
appreciation of the medical staff. Many of those trained by him owed their
subsequent success in their careers to his intolerance of sub-standard work,
although they did not always welcome being on the receiving end of his sharp
tongue. His technician colleagues affectionately knew him as 'The Wee Man'.
Remarkably, it was not until Bert finally retired in 1980 after forty year's
service, that an Ulsterman rather than a Scot headed the technical staff of the
Institute – Jack Reid, who had understudied for years as one of Bert's
assistants. Jack continued the same meticulous and conscientious approach
and thus maintained the superlative standards of tissue preparation and the
introduction of the rapidly expanding technical advances.

Another amazing character was David Mehaffey. David was at first a
hospital porter but was soon promoted to become the mortuary attendant,
and not long thereafter, when John Henry recognised his innate skills, to
the post of photographer for the pathology department. David had no
formal training in photography but had an uncanny knack of modifying the
focus and light intensity to a perfect pitch for the lanternslides projected
during the various teaching sessions. During his career his microphotographs
adorned every M.D. thesis produced by the succession of pathology trainees.

Nevertheless, the nature of the photography facility was extremely intermittent with bursts of intense activity interspersed with many hours of inactivity. David made full use of this leisure time and established contacts during the war with a series of rather dubious traders outside the hospital by which he could overcome the wartime shortages and supplement his own modest salary. Whether it was a rug, a coffeepot, contraceptive, or almost any other article, he could, through his contacts, usually not only provide it but provide it cheaply to students, medical and technical staff. None of his 'customers' dared to inquire whether the articles had 'fallen aff the back of a larry'. Each week John Henry would send him off to get his car filled with petrol thus giving David ample opportunity to ply his alternative trades. It was on one such journey in the 1960s that John Henry's Triumph Renown, Registration OZ 194, finally 'gave up the ghost' and disintegrated in the middle of Shaftesbury Square, causing a massive traffic jam at this busy junction. In the hospital environment everyone knew David and enjoyed sharing his risqué jokes, which were often told with a cigarette dangling from

John Henry at one of the hockey matches (*c.* 1946)
John Edgar Morison is to his left, Yvonne Murray on his right. Also included
are technicians, Albert Lamont front left and Jim Davidson, back right.

his lower lip and interspersed by coughing spasms. He had a rough, bluff exterior combined with a loveable roguish character. These qualities sometimes obscured his underlying heart of gold.

In the mid 1940s and into the 1950s a series of rowdy and so-called 'friendly' hockey matches were arranged between the pathology and bacteriology departments, and also between the laboratory staff and the Royal house officers. Most of the participating players on the laboratory sides, with the exception of Florence McKeown and Yvonne Murray, had never before wielded a hockey stick. This was of no consequence as David Mehaffey, having not the slightest knowledge of the rules, acted as umpire, ensuring that the right team won by blowing on his whistle every time the wrong team threatened to score. John Henry athletically and enthusiastically participated in these games and after one of them wrote an epic poem of many verses entitled 'On ne passe pas' or 'the day that Norman kept his circle' ('Norman' refers to Dr Norman Clotworthy Graham who was appointed first resident Clinical Pathologist at the Royal Victoria Hospital and later became Bacteriologist to the City of Belfast. In 1926 he was appointed lecturer in Bacteriology at the Queens' University. He was affectionately known by generations of medical students as 'Koch' or 'the Hyphe'). Such leisure activities were enjoyed by all and helped weld all the groups of staff into a team prepared to back him to the hilt at work or play.

It often amazed me how my father used his technical staff to carry out mundane duties for him in addition to their laboratory work. For instance, the disabled Louis Bell could sometimes be found 'decoking' my father's pipe with various laboratory chemical solutions. In addition to David Mehaffey's petrol jaunts, two young technicians in the 1940s, Cecil Bennet and, subsequently, Maurice Taggart, each night made the twelve mile return journey by public transport from the Royal Victoria Hospital across to John Henry's home in King's Road in East Belfast, to deliver the tupenny evening newspaper, the *Belfast Telegraph* to my mother. He had also no hesitation in sending a technician to Morris, the newsagent and tobacconist, across the Grosvenor Road from the Institute, for a new packet of Player's No. 3 cigarettes or a tin of Gallagher's Rich Dark Honeydew tobacco to fill his busy pipe.

John Henry's secretary was Thelma Tennis (later Thelma Davidson after marriage), a highly competent typist and organiser. She tried her best to use her feminine wiles to encourage him to reply promptly to the large pile of correspondence that poured on to his desk, but she generally fought a losing battle. My father hated writing letters and preferred to carry on his business by phone or by direct face-to-face discussion. The pile of letters would grow higher and higher until in one fell swoop he would tackle the entire lot on a Saturday morning. He would dictate non-stop to Thelma at high speed leaving her sufficient shorthand to decipher for the next month. This pattern of working meant that there were times when she was virtually redundant and was able, whilst the cat was away, to wander round the hospital and the department having a chat here and a coffee there. She had an arrangement with Colleen Kearney (later on marriage, Colleen Jackson), her counterpart in the Medical Faculty office at Queen's, to give her fair warning of John Henry's imminent return, by phoning the Institute as he was leaving the University.

Slowly but surely, in response to the ever-expanding workload, John Henry eked out funding from the University and hospital to allow a commensurate increase in laboratory staffing. In the 1940s and the early 1950s the pathology department shared the space in the Institute with the other laboratory departments of bacteriology and clinical pathology which incorporated the rapidly developing branches of haematology and biochemistry. Space was at a premium and in response to pressure from the Dean, the University found the money to add a further floor to the building in 1949.

Medical Staffing

On John Henry's arrival in 1937 there were only two young doctors to act as his assistants, Lex Fisher and W. McC. Wilson, and one research fellow, an ex-colonial medical pathologist, Peter Clearkin. John Edgar Morison joined the department as a Musgrave Research student on the same day as my father took up office. He was the last appointment to be made by John Henry's predecessor, Professor J.S. Young, who had resigned to take up the Chair of Pathology in the University of Aberdeen. This tiny nucleus of medical staff was soon to be drastically reduced: Wilson obtained a laboratory post in Coventry; Fisher became an assistant to the Professor of Medicine in Oxford; and Clearkin was recalled to the colonial service. In September 1938 John Edgar Morison and another future star, M.G. (Gerry) Nelson (later to become head of the haematology department in the Royal Victoria Hospital), were appointed as the new pathology demonstrators, the only medical staff now under the guidance of John Henry, and in consequence having to spend long hours carrying out the multifarious hospital and teaching duties of the department, including their own research for the higher degree of M.D. Gerry Nelson's departure in 1940 to join the Royal Air Force Medical Service was followed by the appointment of Tom Milliken, who was later to become a well known consultant physician in the Province. In 1942 John Edgar Morison was upgraded to lecturer with part-time duties to improve the pathology facilities on the Union Hospital site (now the Belfast City Hospital). It was at this stage that he became interested in the reasons for the horrific infant mortality rate, which led later to his internationally renowned book on *Foetal and Neonatal Pathology.**

John Henry was never averse to catching the eye of an attractive girl. There were at that time only a few woman medical students in each year, one reason being the attitude that 'a woman's place was in the home' and the other being the absence of science laboratories in the girls' schools. One day, about 1939, whilst he was demonstrating his post-mortem findings to the students, he noticed an attractive girl trying to avoid being the target of his searching questions by hiding behind one of the pillars that supported the 'Vesalian-styled' mortuary. To her embarrassment he quizzed her on the disease under study. This was Florence McKeown, who was later to follow a distinguished career in pathology and to play a crucial role in the development of the Institute.

John Henry could virtually handpick his assistants from the cream of the medical students available. He did so much of the lecturing himself in the early days that he personally came to know and recognise those who had 'that little bit extra'. They in turn were often flattered to be invited to join 'their' professor's workforce which enhanced their knowledge and also their career prospects. Many notable Ulster doctors passed through the Institute for their postgraduate training. This often entailed working far into the evenings as they struggled with animal experiments for their M.D. research or attended the Journal Club held in John Henry's office each Monday evening. The main part of each day was more than filled by the routine post-mortem examinations, surgical biopsy reporting and student tutorials. Many of these trainees in the 1940s, such as John Edgar Morison, Florence McKeown, Yvonne Murray, Agatha Crawford (eventually a medical

---

* Morison J.E.: *Foetal and Neonatal Pathology*. 1952, 1st, 2nd, 3rd eds. Butterworth, London. 1963, 1965 and 1970. Also published in Italian, Spanish and Japanese.

missionary in China and India), Alwyn Neilly and George Wade (future clinical pathologists in Ballymena and Magherafelt), remained in one or other branch of laboratory medicine. There was also Norman Ainley who was later sadly to die from smallpox, caught whilst he was working in England and conducting an autopsy on a patient with an undiagnosed skin rash (an example of the dangers to which pathologists can be inadvertently exposed). Others, however, stayed only for one or two years in order to complete their M.D. theses or to learn the fundamentals for the practice of some other branch of clinical medicine. John Henry considered pathology the foundation stone for all other medical specialties and could not conceive how anyone could be a good doctor or surgeon if he or she had no understanding of the basis of the disease being treated or resected.

Thus, many of Ulster's well-known doctors spent their early postgraduate years studying pathology. Amongst these were J.W. Sinclair Irwin and Reggie H. Livingstone (consultant surgeons at the Royal Victoria Hospital), J. Frank Pantridge (world famous cardiologist at the Royal), John A. Weaver (metabolic physician at the Royal), and Mary G. (Molly) McGeown (physician responsible for establishing, against extremely difficult odds, the Renal Dialysis and Transplantation Service in Northern Ireland). Frank Pantridge (died 2004) is now known and remembered for his successful fight to establish a 'flying' Cardiac Ambulance Service in Belfast and for helping to pioneer a small mobile defibrillator, an instrument capable of restoring the normal heart rhythm if disturbed following a heart attack. His initial interest in heart disease, however, was developed in the pathology department when he was involved in research into the effects of vitamin B1 (thiamine) deficiency on the cardiac muscle in beri-beri, an interest stimulated by his own harrowing experiences as a Japanese prisoner of war in Malaya. It was entrancing to hear that this most eccentric, brilliant, if at times most difficult consultant, whilst studying for his M.D., could be found in his younger days, on the Institute of Pathology's roof cradling a baby piglet in his arms whilst feeding it a bottle of milk through a teat (He used piglets in his experiments, because pigs were known to have a heart rhythm not unlike humans).

John Henry's attitude to women in medicine is in part revealed by the following story recently related to me by Professor Molly McGeown (died November 2004). She had been working as an assistant in the department and her M.D. thesis on bacterial endocarditis was nearing completion. She had become engaged to Max Freeland, an administrator at Queen's, and they planned to marry soon. She decided to inform John Henry. He was pleased to hear her news but pointed out forcefully to her that by so doing she was barring herself from a career in pathology, as it was not his policy to employ married women. She, typically and equally forcefully, and with considerable nerve, informed him that she had no intention of continuing in pathology and intended to move into clinical medicine! Her decision has brought untold benefit to those in our community who suffer from all forms of kidney disease. Her strong resolve was obviously already in evidence in those early years.

Nevertheless, John Henry did find female doctors who fitted more readily into his chauvinistic criteria for a career in pathology. (It must be remembered that these views were prevalent at that time and that the major changes towards equality of the sexes have only gathered momentum over the last three decades of the twentieth century). Chief among these was Florence McKeown, the initially demure student in the mortuary class. Brought in as an assistant, she was appointed by Queen's to a full-time lectureship in 1943 and rapidly showed her qualities. She and her friend, Yvonne Murray, were the first women appointed to the department. They were both prepared to tackle the arduous tasks and the long hours with eagerness and indeed enjoyment. They even slept on the department floor rather than face the long trip across Belfast during the 'blackout' in the War. Yvonne was to move on after gaining her M.D. to develop her interests in haematology. Florence, however, had found her niche and was to spend the rest of her career in the Institute. Her research into the effects of rheumatic fever on the heart muscle and valves was an extension of studies initiated by Arnold Rich at Johns Hopkins Hospital in Baltimore, one of John Henry's early teachers, and was of innovative importance.

Florence McKeown at her double-headed teaching microscope (c. 1970)

She quickly established a close rapport with my father who recognised her industrious approach to browsing the medical literature and her ability to retain the important facts. Sitting in his office, if not at his feet, she was tutored by him on a tête-à-tête basis as they tackled the diagnostic problems of the autopsies and surgical biopsies. She benefited from this close liaison and eventually became the person, more than any other, on whom John Henry could rely to keep the department functioning smoothly whilst maintaining the high standards that he had introduced. His duties as Dean meant that he had to spend many hours away from the Institute, involved in Medical Faculty administration and innumerable medical committees at the Northern Ireland Hospitals' Authority and at the Department of Health and Social Services at Stormont. The importance of Florence's role cannot be overemphasised. She was the foundation stone on which John Henry's later career flourished. It was not unknown for the cheeks of many a junior trainee pathologist to drain of colour when they heard the approach of her sometimes-strident voice and the brisk sharp click of her high heels echoing on the marble floor of the laboratory corridor. Florence was on the warpath. This usually meant that she had just checked some surgical biopsy or autopsy report and had taken exception to the trainee's wording, grammar or punctuation. Every Saturday, she took home the week's accumulated typed autopsy reports (often thirty or more). Every Monday they were returned with corrections for retyping before they were deemed adequate for issue to the appropriate hospital ward consultant. Such was her attention to detail. Nevertheless, her serious side was more than balanced by her hearty laugh and wonderful sense of humour. Her hair was always beautifully styled as John Henry allowed her to attend the hairdressers twice a week during working hours. This was a very shrewd psychological move on his part, for he knew well that a woman, feeling that she is not looking her best, does not give of her best. She was loved and respected by all the staff and it was recognised that she had an intangible flair – 'feminine intuition'! When some peculiar pattern or rare expression of disease on a microscope slide had defeated all others, it was inevitably Florence who divined the right answer. Even John Henry had eventually to play second fiddle to this talent.

(Florence did eventually get married, one year after her retirement in 1984! She married a widower, Douglas McIwaine, whose first wife, Yvonne (née Murray) had unfortunately died prematurely. As noted previously, Yvonne had been one of Florence's closest life-long friends. Florence then entered the happiest phase of her entire life living in married bliss with Douglas, leaving her professional life behind, and blending effortlessly into the friendship and fellowship of the Killinchy community).

Meanwhile, in 1946 John Edgar Morison had distinguished himself by winning a Rockefeller Fellowship for a year in the Children's Hospital at Harvard University, Boston. On his return in 1947 he was appointed to a full-time lectureship in pathology at Queen's at the Royal Victoria Hospital, whilst Florence McKeown became more responsible for the pathology service to the Belfast City Hospital. As the Geriatric Unit led by Dr (later Professor) George Adams was based on this site, Florence had to perform numerous post-mortem examinations on his very old patients and thus the seeds for another excellent book were sown. She was to publish *Pathology of the Aged** almost twenty years later which was based on her life-time interest in this subject. It was a detailed analysis of 1,500 post-mortem examinations on patients aged between seventy and a hundred years old. Queen's awarded her a D.Sc. in recognition. In 1947 Florence was established as a full-time lecturer in morbid anatomy. In 1953–4 John Edgar Morison was promoted to a readership. He only held this post for a short time before he left the University Department of Pathology to take up a National Health Service consultant post, providing a surgical biopsy and post-mortem service to the hospitals in Northern Ireland outside Belfast. His laboratory was established in one of the old workhouse buildings (Corry's building) on the Belfast City Hospital site. The siting of the laboratory was coincidental and the pathology service to the Belfast City Hospital continued to be provided mainly by the University department at the Royal until 1973. For more than 10 years, John Edgar provided a superb single-handed postal biopsy service to doctors in the rural districts and also found time to travel to the country hospitals to carry out post-mortem examinations on the more puzzling cases. His workload was enormous compared to any other pathology laboratory in the United Kingdom (reaching 16,000 surgical specimens per year; later in 1973 the figure was to rise to a huge 24,000 specimens per year, when the laboratory absorbed the specimens from the City Hospital formerly processed at the RVH laboratory). The University Grants Committee could not believe it when its Medical Sub-Committee visited in 1971. It was not

---

* McKeown, Florence: *Pathology of the Aged*. 1965, Butterworth, London; also published in Australia, Canada, New Zealand, South Africa and USA.

until 1971 that he acquired the able support of another colleague, Dorothy Hayes, soon to be appointed consultant. His reports were noteworthy for the detailed advice, based on his encyclopaedic knowledge, on treatment and prognosis of the rarer diseases. This was of invaluable help to the provincial surgeons who sometimes felt somewhat isolated from the medical libraries and the hub of medical knowledge in Belfast. It was not until the 1960s that good medical libraries were established in the major rural hospitals with linkages to the main University Medical Library. How 'John Edgar' found time to act as a meticulous editor of the *Ulster Medical Journal* from 1954 to 1984 is truly remarkable.

1953–4 saw the debuts of two Queensmen, W.T. Elliott McCaughey and Ross G.S. Malone as temporary lecturers, following the resignation of Jim M. Drennan as lecturer (on his appointment to the Scottish South Eastern Region Hospital Board). Malone eventually left to go permanently to Canada. Elliott McCaughey was appointed a lecturer in applied pathology in 1957–8 but resigned the following year to take up a research post in America. He returned, however, to be re-appointed as a lecturer in the Institute of Pathology in 1961–2. Although colour blind, he was an excellent microscopist and had a restless, inquiring mind so important for the advance of research. His studies into the relationship of the inhalation of asbestos dust and the eventual development of a rare malignant tumour (mesothelioma) of the membranes covering the lungs and the intestine brought him to international attention. In 1963–4 he was successful in his application to the Chair of Pathology in Trinity College, Dublin. There he found considerable resistance to his ideas of centralising the Dublin pathology services which were, at that time, scattered throughout certain city hospitals and run by pathologists who liked to be masters and mistresses of their own domains. They felt that their status would undoubtedly be diminished if they agreed to be absorbed into a more economical and efficient mega-laboratory. He therefore resigned his chair and left for Canada where in 1973 he became Professor and Director of Surgical Pathology in the University of Western Ontario. In 1976 he moved to Ottawa to take up the prestigious post of Director of the Canadian Tumor Reference Centre. In 1986 he joined the Civic Hospital in Ottawa.

In 1955, Dr James B. Gibson, a very competent and genial Scot, filled the lectureship, left vacant after John Edgar Morison's resignation. He had previously served as Surgeon-Lieutenant in the RNVR from February 1944 until October 1946. He had been involved in active service at the Battle of the Atlantic and in the landings in France. On demobilisation in 1946 he had entered the pathology department at the Western Infirmary, University of Glasgow, and had been a lecturer there since 1949. His primary interest was in diseases affecting the liver and he was a competent and informed authority on this subject. He did not always see eye to eye with my father or Florence, but he kept his head down and produced many good publications. He left in 1963 when he became Professor of Pathology in the University of Hong Kong.

The academic year 1958–9 was an important landmark. Up until this time the University Pathology Department, as part of its remit, had dealt with forensic medicine, the branch of pathology related to the legal aspects of, for example, undetermined causes of death. Indeed John Henry revelled in lecturing to his students on subjects such as murder, rape and poisonings. However, there was deemed to be a potential clash in some cases under investigation between hospital, the public interest and the courts. The government therefore called for the establishment of an independent State Forensic Medicine Service. Thus, Thomas K. Marshall arrived on the scene, appointed first as lecturer in forensic medicine within the Institute of Pathology, then in 1960 graded as consultant and as State Pathologist, deriving his salary from both the University and the Ministry of Health and Social Services. He was a tall handsome dogmatic Yorkshireman, who was adept at dealing with Counsel's questioning. His assessments tended to be very black or very white, a stance loved by Counsel. He tolerated no shades of grey, so legal arguments proved easier to sustain. This sometimes brought him into conflict with his Health Service and University pathology colleagues who felt that biological findings did not always allow such positive conclusions and predictions. Tom was a charismatic and popular lecturer. The students packed the lecture theatre to hear him discoursing particularly on the more gruesome aspects of his subject. His department expanded during the 1960s to include Derek Carson, John Press, and trainees such as Abdullah Fateh and Osman Malik. It was, indeed, fortunate that the State pathology service was so well established when the political troubles in Northern Ireland erupted in 1969. Its expertise proved invaluable in the investigation of the many subsequent civilian, military and paramilitary murders. The University Pathology Department could never have coped. Tom's teaching skills were eventually recognised by the University in 1967 when he was appointed an honorary part-time senior lecturer. In later years he was dignified as an Honorary Professor.

Robert Lannigan, a cheerful talkative Scot arrived as senior lecturer in pathology in the mid-1960s. An industrious Hungarian research assistant with veterinary qualifications, Arpad Barabas, who was a research workaholic in the field of immunology, accompanied him. Lannigan was perhaps attracted to Belfast by the prospects of succeeding John Henry, whose retirement in 1971 was beginning to loom. However, he began to think otherwise and instead successfully applied for a Chair of Pathology in Calgary taking his research assistant, Barabas with him.

Throughout the 1950s and 1960s the Institute continued to be the first rung on the career ladder of many well-known, and some not so well-known, doctors in Northern Ireland and further afield. The following long but incomplete table conveys some idea of the remarkable calibre and consistent future success of those lucky enough to be chosen by John Henry to join his department. Each was expected to give his or her all, and more, to help achieve the high standards that he demanded. Each was proud to have been selected and imbued by his infectious enthusiasm for his subject and medicine in general. Each gave him the loyalty that his warm personality inspired.

Future Careers of Trainees in the Institute of Pathology 1940–71

John Edgar Morison	Pathologist to Ulster Provincial Hospitals, Hon. Professor, QUB
Gerry Nelson	Clinical Pathologist, RVH; Hon. Professor of Haematology, QUB
Peter Clearkin	Joined Colonial Service
Lex Fisher	Moved to England to study medicine at Oxford, future career unknown
Florence McKeown	Hon. Professor of Pathology and later Professor of Pathology, QUB
Yvonne Murray	Haematologist, Newtownards Hospital
Agatha Crawford	Medical Missionary, China and India
Frank Pantridge	Cardiac Physician, RVH, Professor of Cardiology, QUB
Alwyn Neilly	Clinical Pathologist, Waveney Hospital, Ballymena
Joe Lowry	Clinical Pathologist, Craigavon Area Hospital
Molly McGeown	Physician in Renal Medicine, BCH, Hon. Professor QUB

Nina Carson	Clinical Biochemist (discoverer of homocystinuria), Dept. of Child Health, QUB
Norman Ainley	Pathologist in England; died prematurely from smallpox
Sinclair Irwin	Consultant Surgeon, RVH
Reggie Livingstone	Consultant Surgeon, RVH
John Weaver	Consultant Metabolic Physician, RVH
Elliott McCaughey	Professor of Pathology, TCD; Professor and Director of Surgical Pathology, University of Western Ontario, Canada
Ross. Malone	Pathologist, St Joseph's Hospital, London, Ontario, Canada
John Bridges	Haematologist, RVH, Professor of Haematology, QUB
Jeffrey Robinson	Clinical Pathologist and Cytologist, BCH
Arthur ffrench O'Carroll	Died prematurely in 1956
Desmond Burrows	Dermatologist, RVH
George Wade	Clinical Pathologist, Mid-Ulster Hospital, Magherafelt
Jeremy Macafee	Consultant Obstetrician and Gynaecologist, Leicester
Jake Willis	Cytologist, RVH; lecturer in Dental Pathology
Ingrid Allen	Professor of Neuropathology, QUB
Harold Jones	Professor of Oral Pathology, University of Manchester
Nigel Reid	Physician in Gastroenterology, Hastings
Hugh Baker	Psychiatrist, England
Derek Carson	Forensic Pathologist, RVH and lecturer QUB
Mary Vint	Dermatological Pathologist, Glasgow
John Ball	Clinical Pathologist, Canada and Hull, England
Alastair Macafee	Orthopaedic Surgeon, MPH
Norman Nevin	Professor of Human Genetics, QUB
Douglas Eakins	Pathologist, King's Lynn, Norfolk, England
Frank McAleenan	Physician, UHD and Downpatrick Hospital
Femi Williams	Professor of Pathology, Lagos, Nigeria
Maurice McLain	Orthopaedic Surgeon, Northampton
Philip Balmer	Radiologist, BCH; radiologist in Brisbane, Australia
Denis Biggart	Pathologist, BCH and Senior Lecturer, QUB
Fred Alexander	Professor of Pathology, University of Calgary, Canada
Douglas Lee	Haematologist in Manchester
Gordon Loughridge	Urosurgeon, BCH
Tom Fannin	Neurosurgeon, RVH
James Ferris	Forensic pathologist, Canada
John Jacques	Pathologist, Canada and Saudi Arabia
Hannan Nagi	Professor of Pathology, Lahore, Pakistan
Raja Sinniah	Professor of Renal Pathology, University of Singapore; Professor of Pathology, Perth, Australia

Denis O' Hara	Paediatric Pathologist, RVH; Senior Lecturer, QUB
Lewis Miller	General Practitioner, East Belfast
James Sloan	Pathologist RVH; Senior Lecturer, QUB
Claire Hill	Renal Pathologist, RVH; Senior Lecturer, QUB
John McClure	Pathologist in Adelaide, Australia; Professor of Pathology, University of Manchester
Philip Mc Kee	Dermatological Pathologist, London; Director of Dermatology in Boston and Associate Professor of Pathology at Harvard Medical School
Ian Craig	Pathologist in Victoria Hospital, London, Ontario and Associate Professor, Department of Medicine, University of Western Ontario, Canada

RVH = Royal Victoria Hospital
BCH = Belfast City Hospital
MPH = Musgrave Park Hospital
UHD = Ulster Hospital, Dundonald
QUB = Queen's University, Belfast
TCD = Trinity College, Dublin

Among the local trainees who remained within the Institute for the rest of their career and deserve special mention were Jacob Willis, Ingrid Allen, Jimmy Sloan, Denis O'Hara and Claire Hill. Jacob made a wonderful job of establishing the Cytology Service at the Royal, whilst Ingrid became an outstanding specialist in Neuropathology and continued to develop John Henry's main research interests. In due course her intellect and talents as a teacher and researcher were rewarded by elevation to a Personal Chair in Neuropathology. Jimmy Sloan was an excellent Histopathologist, particularly interested in Gastroenterological Pathology. The students and junior trainees particularly respected his lecturing, tutoring and good judgment. Similarly, Denis O'Hara in Paediatric Pathology, and Claire Hill in Renal Pathology, both highly regarded, conscientious teachers, made similar important contributions in their subjects.

Others who came more tangentially under his influence because they studied in the Clinical Pathology unit under the leadership of Gerry Nelson, were Dorothy Hayes (Histopathologist at the Belfast City Hospital) and that notable character with her broad North Antrim accent, Betty Nicholl (Clinical Pathologist at Belvoir Park Hospital, Belfast).

First and foremost, John Henry saw himself as a pathologist. To see his department develop and flourish from the scantily staffed unit that he

John Henry, complete with pipe, studying a brain at laboratory bench (*c.* 1955)

had inherited in 1937 filled him with great pride. In spite of his heavy administrative duties in the University he continued for many years to conduct the post-mortem reviews each Wednesday morning in an atmosphere permeated with pungent formaldehyde fumes to which his ever-present pipe seemed to offer immunity. Those crowded around him could scarcely breathe as their eyes and noses streamed. The strict safety regulations of today would not tolerate such conditions. The formaldehyde levels are now closely monitored and no eating or smoking is allowed in the laboratory workplace. John Henry, of course, obeyed only his own rules.

However, towards the end of the 1960–70 decade, recruitment began to be a problem. John Henry was unable to be in the lab as often. He had become more and more involved with the development of the medical school and was fighting for its expansion. He was often away examining or attending Northern Ireland Hospital Authority meetings or the General Medical Council. The clinically orientated academic Department of Medicine at Queen's was diversifying rapidly and the facilities in the adjacent new clinical science block of the University and the professorial units in the hospital itself provided opportunities to carry out interesting laboratory research based on live patients. Many of the brightest young doctors decided to do their M.D. theses in one or other of the specialties under the academic umbrella of 'medicine' rather than in pathology, in which promotional opportunities now seemed limited. Entering medicine protected their interest in clinical patients and allowed them to return to treat patients when their research was complete. They also felt that a career in the pathology laboratory was evolving as a 'back room' job, too isolated from the buzz of the clinical interface. Indeed, this lack of recruitment was a critical factor in my own eventual decision to remain within the environment of pathology for the rest of my working life. I had entered the Institute in September 1961 with the intention of moving to Medicine when my M.D. had been gained. However, strong influences from my father and Florence McKeown were brought to bear on me to stay in the Department. This was one of the most difficult decisions in my life. I was fully aware that if I stayed, I was justifiably open to the criticism of nepotism. However, I had breathed the atmosphere of pathology since childhood and I very much enjoyed the challenges that it presented. I therefore polished my 'brass neck', ignored any adverse whispers, and gingerly placed my tiny feet in the metaphorically gigantic footprints of my father. It was a decision that I rarely regretted throughout my laboratory life. Only on one or two occasions in later life, did the dark shadow of John Henry cause me to ponder my decision.

Throughout John Henry's reign and indeed, thereafter, the Institute remained a hive of activity. Most trainees felt that he expected them to work like 'coolies' and that he had many of the attributes of a slave driver. However, he was not as demanding of them as he was of himself. He had little interest in making the laboratory a place of home comforts. The offices had stark furnishings and hard polished floors on which the wooden chairs scraped noisily. Shortly after his appointment in 1937, he had the office and corridor walls painted a sickly shade of duck-egg green. Throughout the 1940s and into the 1950s the green became even drearier, and if possible, more nauseous as the smoky atmosphere created by his pipe and the numerous little smoky terrace houses of the nearby Grosvenor Road, deposited an ever-darkening layer of grime. In 1950 with the addition of the new floor, his colleagues at last prevailed on him to redecorate and to brighten up the place with a repaint. Once again he chose the original shade of bilious green.

It was not always easy to get him to keep the instruments of the trade up to date. As the staff steadily expanded, the essential microscopes tended not to increase at the same rate and were not replaced with the more streamlined and optically improved models. Old brass mono-ocular microscopes were still being used in the late 1950s when they should really have been presented to the Belfast Museum. This failing on his part was almost certainly due to his possession of an overabundance of fairness. Money as always was scarce. When it became available to the Medical Faculty, he often in his capacity as Dean allocated it to the development of other medical specialties. Those in the pathology department felt that he sometimes tended to overdo the fairness at their expense!

* * * * * * * * * * *

During the week before Christmas, the surgical biopsies tended to decline as the surgeons wound down their work rate, even if the post-mortems remained high. The staff started to prepare for the Christmas festivities. The medical staff had their party and the technical staff had theirs. This separatism would probably not be countenanced today, but John Henry was brought up with the tradition that each group would enjoy itself more amongst its peers. The medical party was organised by the trainees. A table in the corridor groaned with assorted beverages, mostly alcoholic. The large tea table was decorated with the highest quality cutlery and glassware, usually brought in by Florence McKeown. Meanwhile a large tutorial room had been converted into a temporary kitchen. The chef in the Royal Victoria Hospital took care of cooking the turkey, but the rest of the fare was under the control of the pathology staff. Sizzling sausages and bacon were fried over Bunsen burners. Brussels sprouts were peeled and popped into large saucepans; potatoes boiled and mashed; gravies and sauces prepared; plum puddings heated and cream-laden trifles mixed. After an abundance of aperitifs had been consumed, the turkey was summoned from the kitchen vaults of the hospital. John Henry was duly presented with a mortuary knife by Bert Russell and used all his pathological skills to carve for the entire assembly. Fortunately, the knife was always brand new. The feast was duly and noisily consumed amidst much revelry, before those still capable did the washing up whilst lustily singing their repertoire of carols.

In the mid-1960s, there was one party when one of the assistants, John Ball, offered to cut costs and to acquire the turkey from a farmer friend. The turkey duly arrived but unlike the usual one from the butcher, it had not been previously cleaned out. This, of course, presented not the slightest hindrance to a posse of pathologists. However, during the subsequent evisceration, multiple tiny yellow dots were noted in the bird's liver. To satisfy the curiosity of the trainees, frozen sections of the liver were quickly taken and microscopically studied. The sections revealed the lesions to represent infection by avian tuberculosis. Even case-hardened pathologists could not face the prospect of eating the meat and a messenger was quickly dispatched for a prepared replacement from the up-market grocers, Sawers, in Castle Street at the foot of the Falls Road.

Chapter 9

Blood transfusion

The infancy of blood transfusion in Northern Ireland was nurtured by Dr Thomas Houston (later Sir Thomas Houston) who was also responsible for steering the early development of Clinical Pathology at the Royal Victoria Hospital (Haematology and Microbiology).* He had learned his skills whilst treating wounded soldiers in the First World War and set up a voluntary Blood Transfusion service in which he personally took blood from a few hundred voluntary donors. Under his supervision hospital patients were transferred from the wards to the laboratory for transfusion. There were only a few volunteer donors so transfusions in the 1920s and 1930s remained fairly limited.

It was in 1939 with the Second World War looming, that John Henry assumed a prominent role in establishing the Emergency Blood Transfusion Service. At that time the hospitals depended for their relatively few transfusion episodes on the good will of the local branch of 'Toc H' or the individual efforts of harassed house officers as they tried to persuade relatives and visitors to be volunteer donors. The importance of blood typing into the four groups O, A, B and AB, was then recognised (the M, N, P groups and the Rhesus and other factors came later) but too often blood was blood and transfusion catastrophes of incompatible blood types were not uncommon. However, in the atmosphere of war-time it was not difficult to find recruits, and visits to the large firms of the city rapidly increased the enrolment of donors. Yet it was curious where the enthusiasm prevailed. Woolworth's staff had virtually 100% enrolment whilst Harland and Wolffs', the world-renowned ship building firm, then under a reactionary management, refused to grant admission; employees who volunteered had to do so in their own

---

* *Pathology at the Royal. The First Hundred Years 1890–1990.* Published 1990: The Royal Group of Hospitals.

time as was also to be the case in the 1950s with the Mass Miniature Radiography (MMR) screening programmes. When the first blitz hit the city on Easter Tuesday, 15th April 1941, it was therefore very possibly anaemic counter girls of Woolworths who contributed the first replacements to the rapidly depleting store in the blood banks. John Henry found it curious how people reacted to giving a blood sample. After a Rotary Club lunch the percentage of faints was about ten, while a line of sailors from a then visiting warship rolled over one after the other. Indeed the only time John Henry was knocked off his feet was by a six-foot sailor falling over him after he had taken a small blood sample. For publicity purposes the Lord Mayor bared his arm, the photographer's shutter clicked, but before my father could drive the needle into his vein the mayoral cuff links were hastily refastened. However, the campaign was successful, though it meant many hours of driving in the blackout and returning home at midnight or thereafter. On one occasion he returned home distraught after knocking down and injuring a cyclist. Car headlights at the time were covered by black grills, which threw only a low intensity beam on to the road, and had failed to illuminate the shadowy cyclist whose injuries, fortunately, were not serious. Eventually his team was able to establish a 'bleeding' bus in which it was possible to bleed donors, refrigerate the bottles of blood and return them to the main blood bank. In this way the volunteering enthusiasm of the small country town and village inhabitants was given expression.

My father was proud of the role played by the Queen's medical students and came to recognise that they had been given insufficient praise for their efforts during the war. In the blood transfusion service there was virtually 100% recruitment, far in excess of that among students in the other faculties. He and his mainly student team developed a chain system of alert in case of emergency and so when he phoned four students he knew that the whole system would be alerted. When, eventually, the first massive air-raid occurred (in April 1941) it was impossible for him not to be full of pride as student after student turned up, all with their four donors. Some of the students were bandaged or plaster-splinted after having been dug out of demolished houses but, fit or injured, each and every one produced his or her quota of donors. There were, of course many unforeseen difficulties such as when it was realised that the special paraffin lamps, with which each student had been issued in case of electrical failure, made it almost impossible to see a vein. So each had to learn to locate and penetrate the veins by touch alone.

It was the achievements and enthusiasm of the students that made it difficult for my father to be completely objective in assessing their subsequent examinations. During the war the number of blood transfusions increased six-fold and many blitz casualties, as well as surgical and medical cases in the hospital wards, owed their lives to the existence of the transformed blood transfusion service.

Whilst the Ministry of Health had designated John Henry as Blood Transfusion Officer, he was given no funds to create a service. So the bleeding sessions held each week were manned entirely by the assistant medical staff of the laboratory. Eventually he succeeded in obtaining for them a small sessional fee, but it was their intense commitment to the war effort and perhaps some loyalty to him personally that led to their considerable contribution to the success of the service which in the air-raids on Belfast during 1941 was not found wanting. The Northern Ireland Blood Transfusion Service operated as a wartime emergency measure under the direction of John Henry until 1946 when, acting on his advice, the Ministry of Health and Local Government established the service on a permanent basis and assumed full administrative, executive and financial responsibility for it until the inception of the National Health Service (NHS) in 1948, when these were transferred to the new Northern Ireland Hospitals Authority (NIHA). Thereafter the laboratory aspects of blood transfusion were separated from that of donor recruitment and blood collection. The Blood Transfusion Laboratory was directed by Dr Clare Huth and was at first housed in the Royal Victoria Hospital, before moving to the Belfast City Hospital in 1961; and eventually, in 1970 to refurbished facilities in Durham Street. The administrative headquarters and blood donor organisation began at Ministry of Health offices in Tyrone House, Ormeau Avenue before moving to Howard Street (1953). Amalgamation of the laboratory and administrative sides in one location did not occur until 1970 when it was finally achieved under the direction of Colonel Tom E. Field (Dr Huth's successor after her retirement). It is remarkable how the Blood Transfusion Service which started as a tiny offshoot of Haematology, has grown and developed throughout the twentieth century into a speciality in its own right. Modern medicine and surgery relies heavily on its support. Since 1995 Belfast is most fortunate in having a large, modern, purpose-built building on the Belfast City Hospital site, incorporating all aspects of the service.

* * * * * * * * * * *

For political reasons conscription was not applied to Northern Ireland. From a medical standpoint this had its disadvantages. Whilst British medical schools were enabled to reserve the call-up of medical men, this did not apply to Northern Ireland; many recent graduates, usually after a basic minimum time in hospital, then enlisted with the forces and moved away (the compulsory Pre-Registration House Officer Year was not introduced until 1953). A few women doctors covered not one hospital ward unit, but two. Graduates, who my father had marked as capable of a future stellar career, died in Egypt or elsewhere on what seemed at the time fatuous exercises. In the last throes of the Malaya campaign, up to and including the fall of Singapore, Ulster medicine lost, through death or capture, some of the cream of Queen's medical graduates. Yet others survived to return to successful, even prestigious practice Thomas Boyd Smiley, MC, consultant thoracic surgeon, RVH and Frank Pantridge, MC, at once come to mind and the spirit of the medical school was high, only shaken on the day when the French capitulated between the examination papers on pathology and therapeutics. John Henry sent those who were unsuccessful back to try again because he knew that they would only too soon be needed at the war front.

To the students of those years my father could not pay sufficient tribute. Night after night they manned the roof tops of the hospitals – with the exception of the Mater Infirmorum where the Mother Superior refused them access to the roof, not because she ignored the need or spurned their offer, but because it meant passing through the sleeping quarters of the nurses. Curiously, the only incendiary bomb to fall on a hospital fell on the Mater Hospital! John Henry remembered doing a round of the rooftops of the Royal Victoria Hospital at 3 a.m. and finding behind each little pinnacle a group of card-playing students. They were happy though their only light was a shaded torch and their pint of beer could only be found by touch outside the limited circle of light.

In 1948 my father was appointed C.B.E. for his part in 'organising the Blood Transfusion Service and emergency medical services in Northern Ireland'.

Chapter 10

Student mentor and teacher

Introduction

In an earlier chapter I have referred to the students' tradition of holding 'rags' for newly appointed professors and notable political visitors. There was to be no escape for John Henry when he first took up his professorship at Queen's in 1937. After his first few lectures, he was duly warned to turn up next day in old clothes. Clad in a white surgical gown and crowned with his old school cap he was placed by the students in a barrel on a dray-cart and duly led from the hospital to Queen's University via the grounds of his old school, RBAI. Some three hundred high-spirited medical students noisily accompanied the cart with a praetorian guard of senior students surrounding the barrel who took the brunt of the flying tomatoes, which the various fruit shops on the way relinquished all too readily. Once on the University campus a team of student 'pathologists' took control and performed a mock autopsy. From John Henry's covering sheet they produced a 'heart of stone' and yards and yards of entrails, which were in fact long strings of uncooked sausages. These 'organs' were then passed to a team of presiding soothsayers, who seemingly bore more than a superficial resemblance to three eminent professors in the Faculty of Arts. Having carefully studied the offered 'entrails' with serious intent, the seers pronounced the omens as favourable and the student body accepted John Henry into its midst.

* * * * * * * * * * *

In the late thirties and throughout the forties, the paucity of teaching staff meant that everyone had a heavy teaching load. My father shouldered much of the lecturing himself and also the brunt of an ever-increasing surgical biopsy and autopsy service. As a beneficial result he came to know the character, strengths and weaknesses of every medical student in the department. In later years he often rued the loss of this affinity with his

John Henry being ragged by Queen's students (1937)

John Henry undergoing post-mortem in front of Queen's University during his initiation
by students. Strings of intestines (sausages) are being pulled from his body (1937)

John Henry with staff and medical students in front of Institute of Pathology.
On his right is John Edgar Morison, two to his left is student Florence McKeown.
Gerry Nelson is peeping over her shoulder (1939)

students as staff numbers steadily increased and, somewhat reluctantly he was able to delegate more of his increasing workload. It was for this reason that his fondest memories were of his first thousand students encountered over his first ten years in post. After this the University granted him his first lecturer.

John Henry loved lecturing and teaching. He seemed to have inherited a natural talent, perhaps from his teacher parents. Each year a new group of students arrived at the Royal Victoria Hospital, full of enthusiasm and avid for clinical knowledge, having successfully surmounted the hurdle of the 2nd professional examination in anatomy, physiology and biochemistry. At their first pathology lecture they came face to face with their Dean (my father was elected Dean of the Medical Faculty in 1944), who most had not seen since he had interviewed them for admission to the Medical School. In that first lecture, he would seek out the students who had won the Symington Medal in Anatomy and the Milroy Medal in Physiology. Others at risk of selection were those who had studied Latin and Greek. He would then, to the relief and amusement of the others, expose the gaps in these students' knowledge by asking them some obscure questions. Thereafter he was assured of total attention since no student dared risk the possibility of an inquisition.

Whenever possible and certainly during his first ten years as professor, he arranged to give most of the lectures himself. He thought it a privilege to teach the ex-servicemen returning from the Second World War who, in contrast to those from the First World War, intended to qualify in the shortest possible time and, being older, added maturity to the mix with their younger associates. After the war the number of assistants in the pathology department gradually grew and those such as Florence McKeown, James Gibson, Elliott McCaughey and John Edgar Morison undertook more lectures. However, he was still giving most of the lectures himself when I was one of his students in 1958 and 1959.

On three days each week during the university term he was usually available at 11.00 a.m. to give the introductory lecture to the third year medical students on the basic principles of disease mechanisms. This was followed, at 12.15 p.m., by a lecture to the fourth year students on a specific disease entity as part of the combined clinical curricular course. In the short interval between each lecture he would return to his nearby office with the intention of gathering his thoughts and putting his slides for the next lecture into order, but these hopes were often dashed because his senior clinical colleagues, such as Professors Macafee and Rodgers and Mr (later Sir) Ian Fraser had learned that this was the best time to entrap him on site to seek advice on their own pressing clinical administrative problems. He would therefore often be slightly late for the second lecture: but he would descend the steps to the rostrum; the back doors would close, and beware any student who arrived still later because he or she would then be invited down to the front bench to be peppered with questions during the lecture.

Today, with the development of educational trainers, some attempt is being made to help lecturers to teach and communicate their message – a long overdue necessity for many. One of their edicts is that one should stand motionless at the rostrum as one seeks to inspire the audience. Not so John Henry! He had no need for a rostrum; all his notes were stored in his head. As he lectured he strode backwards and forwards, like a caged lion, across the front of the lecture theatre with his head slightly bowed as if seeking and deriving inspiration from his moving feet. Occasionally he would face his captive audience as with a combination of flowing words and dramatic hand gesticulations, he conjured up a vivid image of, perhaps, a tawny cirrhotic liver or a syphilitic aortic aneurysm or a spongy lung solidified by pneumonia. As the pearls of wisdom cascaded, most students were held enthralled as they tried to capture them in their notebooks for later regurgitation at the exams. He had of course already impressed on them that the study of the mechanisms of disease (i.e. pathology) was the essential foundation on which their future careers in medicine depended, no matter which specialty they later chose to follow. The female students were particularly conscientious in note-taking and on occasions were so enrapt that they continued to write furiously as John Henry injected one of his not infrequent and often slightly risqué jokes. One such story that he ended a lecture (with his usual accompanying dramatic portrayal of the picture with gesticulations) went something like this:

> Once upon a time a little girl was born with a golden screw in her umbilicus. As she grew up into a beautiful teenager and began to take an interest in boys, she became more and more upset and self-conscious about this defect which marked her as different from her other girl-friends. (Today with all the decorative pins and beads piercing teenagers' bodies, she would have had no such problem). She sought advice and help far and wide and eventually located a very wise man. He explained that she could have the screw removed if, at the time of the next full moon, she lay down naked on her bed beside the open window and allowed the moon to shine on her tummy.
>
> On the next full moon she duly carried out the wise man's instructions and lay on her back with the bright moonlight playing on her naked, nubile, body and highlighting the glistening golden screw. For a long time nothing untoward happened, but at the stroke of midnight a little goblin, carrying a tiny golden screwdriver, slid down a moonbeam on to her tummy. He inserted the screwdriver, which was exactly made to measure, into the groove in the little golden screw and ever so slowly began to turn it in an anticlockwise direction until it was fully loose. Then with his tiny fingers he carefully lifted it out of her navel and ... HER BOTTOM FELL OFF!

By 1948 his reputation as a teacher was well and truly established. The students recognised that here was a professor with their interests at heart. He was their mentor and earnestly wanted each of them to succeed in his or her future medical career. It was in this year that the date of his birthday leaked out and the students decided that the occasion should not be missed

John Henry drinking his whiskey at his birthday party, urine bottle is convenient. His cake is brain-shaped. Behind him is student, Denis Boyle (now retired cardiologist) (*c.* 1956)

as a golden opportunity to release their more basic animal spirits. On the 17th November 1948 when John Henry arrived at the lecture theatre he found it in Stygian gloom relieved only by the flickering candles on a birthday cake. He descended the steps to the front of the lecture theatre to a hearty, if not particularly musical, rendering of 'Happy Birthday, John Henry'. Beside the cake was a tumbler filled to the brim with neat Irish whiskey. In front of him were a hundred or more clamouring students who refused to stop shouting until he had emptied the glass. They were then content to sit back and listen to his lecture expecting it to disintegrate into a slurred and illogical account as his blood alcohol level rose. They were to be disappointed for although my father had never before imbibed such a quantity of neat whiskey so quickly he had a very hard head, and plenty of practice. Indeed, as he recounted his version of this episode many years later, he viewed it as a paean of triumph to have, towards the end of his allotted hour, flawlessly pronounced the tongue-twisting 'there is no *one* poliomyelitis; there are the poliomyelit-id-es.' Actually this was more a prophecy than a fact for at that time the various strains of the responsible virus had not yet been clearly identified.

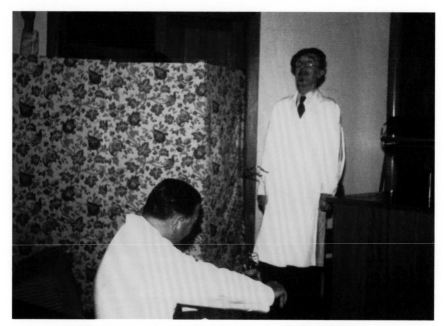

John Henry watching his birthday party show with amusement.
Louis Bell, technician, is included as a Frenchman, complete with beret (*c.* 1956)

In this mild and modest fashion began an annual celebration which grew into a momentous annual event known as 'the Dean's birthday party'. Each year he would be presented with a bottle of whiskey and a birthday cake which in later years was always a work of art: once it assumed the shape of a convoluted marzipan brain; another time it was modelled as his book of Neuropathology; and on yet another occasion as the scarlet red face of the Dean himself, complete with heavy eyebrows and trim moustache. The huge lecture theatre became packed to the doors with an audience that not only included all three years of clinical medical students but also hospital medical staff and off-duty nurses from the Royal Victoria Hospital corridor, as well as supposedly on-duty laboratory staff of all grades. The whole session often lasted several hours. As the percentage of female students steadily increased there was often an accompanying dance routine with a line of high-kicking and scantily clad chorus girls who would have given the Blue Bell Girls a run for their money. One year the theme was 'THIS IS YOUR PATHOLOGY, JOHN HENRY' based on the popular BBC show compèred by Eamon Andrews. A student dressed in a dinner suit and bow tie ushered John Henry to an armchair. Under the student's arm was a book supposedly filled with the important milestones in my father's life. Slides were projected, one of which depicted him starting out in life as a foetus lying within the womb, his passage to the outer world obstructed by his large eyebrows (apparently the first known case of eyebrow praevia). The foetal professor was portrayed as receiving nourishment from a whiskey bottle poured into his umbilical cord. Was the foetal skin yellow on account of perinatal jaundice or was the alcohol already having an affect on his liver?

As the years passed 'The Dean's Birthday Party' became more of a bawdy variety concert and an opportunity for the students to mimic, with pungent humour, the eccentricities and weaknesses of their hospital teachers. For example, the Professor of Therapeutics and Pharmacology, Owen Wade, who had a rather large mouth with puffy lips, was on one such occasion mimicked by a student, John McClure (later to become Professor of Pathology at the University of Manchester). McClure depicted Professor Wade as the only man who could eat a Mars bar sideways and proceeded to confirm this fact to the astounded audience. And there were many other impersonations. Although this portrayal of a teacher's defect may seem cruel to the general public, those bearing the brunt of the humour usually displayed their good sportsmanship and laughed at themselves. They realised that to be impersonated by their students was an indication that they were held in affection; it was those teachers who were not impersonated who had to ask themselves what they were doing wrong.

When the show ended to the strains of 'Happy Birthday,' John Henry would rise to his feet amidst much cheering which quickly gave way to an almost eerie hush. With a beaming smile spread across his rubicund face, he would first graciously thank the organisers and performers and comment on how he was glad to see that the animal spirits of medical students were still as rampant as

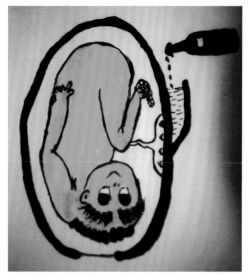

John Henry depicted in utero as first case of 'eyebrow praevia', nourished through umbilical cord by whiskey (c. 1956)

ever. He would then become serious and emotional. Holding his audience spellbound, he would launch into a philosophical treatise on what being a doctor meant to him and how privileged those who studied medicine were to be able to give succour to members of society in their weakest hours – their hours of illness. He called on each of his students to prosper by applying to their future medical careers the 'The Three Loves' of Hippocrates, the ancient Greek (*c.* 3000 BC) known as the 'Father of Medicine'. These were *philosophia* (the love of wisdom), *philotechnia* (the love of the art), and the greatest of the three – *philanthropia* (love of one's fellow man). As he finished and left the arena to a standing ovation, not a few could be seen surreptitiously brushing away a tear, including on occasions my father himself.

When the results of the final year exams became available, John Henry insisted in following a ritual, not practiced by other faculties. He would emerge directly from the Examiners' Meeting into the Queen's University quadrangle to face the group of nervously expectant final year medical and dental students. He then read out the names in alphabetical order followed by the tag of either Pass or Fail. Most students fell into the Pass category and the relaxation of tension was immediately tangible. The few who failed to make the grade faded quickly and quietly from the scene to lick their wounds and try again the following year. The most timid of the students did not face up to this ordeal, but crept surreptitiously up to the Academic notice board several hours later and viewed the listed results without fear of embarrassment. This custom soon faded out after John Henry's retirement.

It was obvious that he took immense pleasure in seeing his students graduate after their years of toil, trials, and tribulation. A feature of the day was a photograph of the entire graduating year in their academic regalia with John Henry sitting in their midst. Before the graduation ceremony he insisted on them taking a modernised version of the ancient Hippocratic Oath. This modification was known as the 'Sponsio Academica'. In unison the new doctors had to repeat the following words:

> I do solemnly declare that as a graduate in Medicine of The Queen's University of Belfast, I will exercise my profession to the best of my knowledge and ability for the good of all persons whose health may be placed in my care and for the public weal; that I will not knowingly or intentionally do any thing or administer any thing to any person to their hurt or prejudice for any consideration or motive

whatsoever; that I will hold in due regard the honourable obligations of the medical profession doing nothing inconsistent therewith; and I do also declare that I will keep silence about those things which I have seen or heard while visiting the sick; and I do further declare that I will be loyal to my University and endeavour to promote its welfare and maintain its traditions.

John Henry's interest in his students did not cease after their qualification. He retained an acute interest in their future careers and successes. Many continued to send him Christmas cards and letters from all over the globe. When he learned of the premature death of any of the graduates he felt it keenly. The deaths of Dinah Kohner and 'Mo' Taylor touched him particularly deeply. Both were lovely girls cut off in their prime. Dinah, when aged only two years, and her family had migrated to Belfast from Czechoslovakia in 1938 before the Second World War. She was a brilliant, Gold Medal (Ulster Hospital) winning student of bubbling vitality whose enthusiasm affected and infected all those around her, including her teachers and John Henry himself. Her tragic death from a subdural haematoma following a plane crash in Ecuador during international work for impoverished children of the third world, deprived society of a deeply caring doctor. In her memory a charitable fund was set up, to be used for research into diseases of children, with a special emphasis on leukaemia. 'Mo' was a different sort of character, equally loved by her fellow students and teachers. Always cheerful she was a bundle of kindness and softness. Unfortunately she was stricken by a life-threatening cardiac illness a few years after qualification, which was diagnosed not long after her marriage to Alan Crockard, a neurosurgeon at the Royal Victoria. She faced her illness with tremendous fortitude and by devoting most of her hours to charitable causes. In this extract from his panegyric for 'Mo', there emerged the deep, complex, emotional side of John Henry with his intense feeling of loss for, as he would have seen it, one of the lambs in his flock:

> Yet it is not merely for her medical career that we shall remember her. Rather it will be for that delightful personality, that effervescent cheerfulness, and her obvious devotion and dedication to her chosen profession.

'The fairest things have the fleetest end'

Like the ideal wife of whom Plutarch speaks – the best doctor is often the one of whom the public hears least. Her ways were ways of gentleness.

Always she evinced a humanity that showed in her daily life, a tenderness and consideration to the weak, an infinite pity to the suffering, and broad charity to all. She found great happiness, for happiness lies in absorption in others, in some vocation that satisfies the soul.

In everything she exhibited that Hippocratic probity which made her under all circumstances true to herself, true to the high calling of her profession, and true to her fellow men and women.

Courage and cheerfulness carried her over the rough places of life, and enabled her to bring healing, and if not healing at least comfort and ease to the suffering sons and daughters of man.

For 34 years she gave of herself to this world, brought happiness to her parents and the family circle, love to her husband, and life and laughter to her friends. None of this has been misspent. There can be no bitter after-taste. The world is a better place because of what she did, and was.

So though we mourn, let us also give thanks:

> Good-bye: No tears or cries are fitting here, and long lament were vain
> Only the last low words be softly said,
> And the last greeting given above the dead.
> Sleep after toyle, port after stormy seas,
> Ease after warre, death after life. Does greatly please.
>
> Spenser

* * * * * * * * * * *

Sir William Osler, the supreme philosopher-physician, stated that 'the hardest conviction to get into the mind of a beginner is that the education upon which he is engaged is not a college course, but a medical course, ending only with death, for which the work of a few years under teachers is but a preparation'. John Henry idolised Osler and his philosophy. He bought the second edition (1929) of his book *Counsels and Ideals** just after his appointment to the Chair of Pathology in Belfast and often quoted from its pages during his lectures and talks. Just as the medical student must continue to study after attaining his medical degree, so John Henry continued to teach with relish those who were now termed post-graduates, but in his eyes remained his students.

Within his own department he took delight in passing on his in-depth knowledge of disease to his pathology trainees. At first, when the staff was sparse, he did this on a tête-à-tête basis, showing and expounding on the intricacies of each rare or puzzling biopsy picture down his microscope. As the trainees increased in number he established an in-house class of trainees. This was designated as 'The Red Star' class which developed into a much feared but very educational ritual. It was held each Friday morning. Selections of slides from the most difficult or rare cases of the previous week were collected in two black boxes, one from the laboratory of the City Hospital and one from the Royal Victoria. The boxes were interchanged between the two labs midway through the week. All consultant pathologists and trainees were expected to study the sections during the week and come to the class with their opinions formed and ready to describe and attempt to deduce logically the correct diagnoses. There was perhaps a little prior lateral discussion of the cases amongst those trainees of the same stage. It was, however, considered *verboten* to help those from a more junior year with less experience: they were left to struggle through numerous pathology tomes in an effort to unravel the mysteries in the hope that they would not seem too stupid or ill-informed. When the class assembled there was a hush as John Henry, Florence McKeown and John Edgar Morison took up their seats in the front row. The lights went out. The slides of each case were projected onto the screen and John Henry would call for one of the most recent trainees to give his assessment. He sought in turn the views of the second and third year trainees, before he himself pronounced the final diagnosis, no argument brooked. And so to the next case! It could be a terrifying experience for the more timid, but it was a wonderful way to learn and indelibly impress a picture in the memory for a lifetime. This was particularly

---

* Osler, William: *Counsels and Ideals*. 1929 2nd ed. Humphrey Milford, Oxford University Press London, Toronto, Melbourne, Capetown, Bombay, Calcutta, Madras, Shanghai.

so if one's answer received the 'thumbs down' from John Henry. The other value of the class was that every pathologist in the two hospitals had had the opportunity to view and discuss all the most interesting cases passing through both labs.

There was one occasion when the almost inconceivable happened. During 'The Red Star', John Henry barked out the name 'Douglas'. There was no answering voice from the dark. 'Douglas', this time John Henry's voice was sharper and louder. Suddenly, there was a screeching of a wooden chair on the polished composite floor followed by a dull thump: Douglas Lee had fallen off his chair after having had the temerity to fall fast asleep in 'The Red Star', whilst others trembled.

Perhaps my father's greatest teaching achievement was the establishment of the so-called Lab Meetings, more formally 'Clinico-Pathological Conferences'. Such were their reputation that hospital clinicians, general practitioners and pathologists flocked to the practical room of the Institute of Pathology not only from the Belfast area but even at times from as far away as Ballymena. The meetings were held at 4.45 p.m. on alternate Wednesdays from the autumn to the end of spring. They often lasted until 6.30 or even 7.00 p.m. Each meeting comprised a series of about four interesting topical cases based on the post-mortem findings or on a recent biopsy report. The clinician associated with a particular case was asked to give a brief account of the patient's symptoms on admission to hospital and the reasons for the diagnosis made. The appropriate trainee pathologist would then present the autopsy or biopsy findings and give a dissertation on the condition. This was another nerve-racking experience. The trainee had often been given but a few days to research in depth the disease under review. He or she was expected to have probed and digested the world literature and be in a position to answer questions from the experienced audience. John Henry would under no circumstances allow the trainee to use notes. The presentation had to be extempore. The trainee faced front rows packed with the most senior hospital physicians and surgeons, all of whom had shortly before been his or her teachers and examiners. The questions could be difficult and sometimes tinged by the scepticism of an unbelieving clinician. The trainee would often know more than the inquisitor on account of his recent reading of the relevant literature, but should John Henry sense that his pathologist was in difficulties, he would immediately jump up from the front row to protect his trainee. He would turn to face the audience and give an unprepared talk, often a tour-de-force, on the condition based on other similar cases that he had encountered during his career and based on his extensive reading and on his remarkably retentive memory. Even the most persistent and cynical clinician fell silent as John Henry then proceeded to conduct events and used his meeting to enlighten subtly the entire audience in the most recent advances in the knowledge of the condition in question. For the trainee presenter it was an invaluable experience for confidence building. He or she learned to speak without notes and if there was a stumble it was not too critical as the atmosphere was basically friendly and supportive. Later in one's career the confidence would pay off when such presentations were made to national and international conferences.

Chapter 11

Faculty of Medicine

After his appointment to the Chair of Pathology in 1937, John Henry quickly impressed his medical colleagues of his administrative talents despite his being only thirty-one. His forceful enthusiasm, negotiating skills and driving ambition for the success of the Medical School were quickly recognised and he was soon acting as *de facto* scribe at the Faculty meetings, the minutes of which, in the early 1940s, were in his own handwriting. His medical colleagues would frequently bracket his name with that of the Dean and more senior professors, to be delegates in representation to the Vice-Chancellor in important matters, especially of finance.

In 1944 the Dean, William J. Wilson, Professor of Public Health, who had served the Faculty as its Dean for fourteen years, though not due to retire from his chair for another three years, intimated that he would not seek re-election. John Henry was at once elected in his place for the year 1944–5, being proposed and seconded by the two senior members, C.G. Lowry, Professor of Midwifery (1920–23) and also of Gynaecology (1937–45), and by William (later Sir William) W.D. Thomson, Professor of Medicine (1923–50), and he chaired his first Faculty meeting on 19th September 1944. Little did he realise that he would be re-elected each year for an uninterrupted period of 27 years until his retirement, his final meeting being on the 29th June 1971. It is a measure of the primacy he gave to the Faculty that although these meetings took place eight or nine times every year, he chaired all except four over this entire period: two were chaired by Professor Macafee as acting Dean in 1962, (when John Henry was recuperating from his gallbladder operation); another was chaired by Professor Douglas Harrison on 3rd November 1964 (when John Henry was re-visiting USA with a professorial team to study recent developments in medical education in Columbia University, and the Albert Einstein Medical Centre, New York, as well as Cleveland University, Boston University and his former training centre at Johns Hopkins University, Baltimore); and one by Professor Peter Froggatt, the Dean-elect, on 27th April 1971.

The Deanship was subject to annual election by the Faculty and each year John Henry would be re-nominated by Professor Douglas Harrison or, after Harrison's retirement, by Professor Harold Rodgers, and elected unopposed, and each time he would graciously thank Faculty for its continued confidence and support for him and agree to serve for another year. The interrelationship between John Henry, as Dean, and his Faculty colleagues was one that generally suited them both. His colleagues soon recognised that he was a man of vision, energy and good sense, intent on placing the Queen's Medical School on the national and international map. In 1951, following the death of Professor W.W.D. Thomson, Faculty recommended to the University that my father should fill the resultant vacancy of Queen's representative on the General Medical Council in London, and he continued in this role, even after his retirement in 1971, right up to his sudden death in 1979 in Brown's Hotel in London, while on General Medical Council business.

Faculty members, who numbered along with the academic staff members many part-time 'clinical teachers' and examiners, perceived him as fair and broad-minded and prepared to argue and fight the battles on their behalf. They all learned to trust and respect him implicitly and realised that it was to their benefit to accept him as the 'benign dictator' as by instinct he clearly was and in practice soon became. John Henry, on the other hand, derived great satisfaction from wielding such power and influence and being put in a

John Henry with a spring in his step revisiting USA (1964)

117

position from which he could strive to fulfil his dreams of a vibrant Medical School of international reach. He strove to make the standards equal or better than those in Britain and comparable with all but the very best of those in the United States of America.

Most of his hard work was invisible. Behind the scenes he would discuss the problems of the moment and thrash out their answers with the various professors, on an individual basis, prior to the Faculty meetings. He would consult 'the powers that be' at university, teaching hospital and Ministry of Health levels in his efforts to move things forward. The Agenda, a 'skeleton' affair, was only circulated at the beginning of each meeting: members attending had no prior opportunity to rehearse any contrary arguments, whilst those not attending were excluded from knowing the topics to be discussed. To complete this 'committeemanship' the minutes of the meeting were recorded in the Minute Book and read out by the Chair or attending secretary at the start of the following meeting: none were ever pre-circulated though the Minute Book was (just about) available for prior consultation, though it rarely was. For each item on the Agenda, he would explain the problem and then put forward his proposed solution. He would then forcibly utter the question – 'Agreed?' Almost without exception, members would reverently murmur and nod in deferential assent. Discussion was invariably minimal and often stifled. If a questioner, a rare breed indeed, persisted, John Henry's weapon which he kept in reserve for such unusual occasions, was simple and effective: he would say 'Good point, Dr So-and-So, but unfortunately the General Medical Council would never allow it'. Since during his lengthy tenure of being both Faculty Dean and Queen's GMC representative no-one else on Faculty had ever been, nor knew just what the GMC did, could do, or how it would do it; this tactic was water-tight. Meetings, which started at 5 p.m., were conducted speedily and efficiently. Dinner was never delayed and John Henry had once more been given carte blanche to travel along his chosen paths which he was convinced would lead to the greatest rewards. It must be said that a few members resented this curtailment of discussion and the imposition of the Chairman's will, and some, particularly amongst the non-academic hospital 'clinical lecturers and examiners', wondered why the meetings were necessary at all, being merely for 'rubber-stamping' John Henry's decisions. One such was the late Dr 'Freddie' Kane who rarely attended but when he did invariably questioned one or more decisions of the Chair. John Henry always listened to Dr Kane with courtesy and apparent attention (possibly because Kane had out-scored him in Final M.B.); but he still got his own way.

At the end of the war in 1945 the student numbers rose sharply with the enrolment of ex-service men wishing to complete their medical studies, but there were also graduates who required the establishment of courses to refresh their knowledge or to study towards higher degrees and qualifications. Whilst these were Faculty responsibilities, the (honorary) medical staffs of the teaching hospitals collaborated with enthusiasm. This close association of the University with the hospitals led to co-operation and a certain integration of their functions and John Henry's genial character and bonhomie played no small part in bringing this about. There was at times some jealousy between the two factions, but this was minimal when compared to the outright antagonism between university and hospital staff that existed in many centres in Britain. The minimum numbers of clinical students and those obtaining post-graduate qualifications were adequately provided for and became the foundation stone of the future success of a medical school, which was to flourish and expand in the following twenty seven years of John Henry's guidance.

The departments of the Medical School benefited from increased government grants following University Grants Committee visits in 1945 and again in 1948, and with the introduction of the National Health Service. There were also contributions from the University Centenary Fund and other, more modest, sources. This finance allowed a very essential increase in the teaching staff. The Nuffield Trust generously funded the establishment of a Chair in Child Health. The part-time Chair of Public Health, which had just been vacated by Professor William J. Wilson, the previous Dean, was transformed into the full-time Chair of Social and Preventive Medicine. The Faculty of Medicine had since 1922 also been responsible for the School of Dentistry which had survived in spite of extremely poor funding and inadequate housing. In 1948 its position was strengthened by the appointment of Philip Stoy to a new full-time Chair of Dentistry and of James Scott to a lectureship in Anatomy for dental students. Furthermore, Professor Stoy was elected Deputy Dean of the Faculty of Medicine and year by year, like John Henry, he was successfully re-elected. My father and Stoy worked together in relative harmony throughout their working careers and this allowed the Dental and Medical Schools to develop and expand together. There were, however, a few clashes, when my father's biased views surfaced. In his eyes Medicine attracted altogether superior types of human being; full of loving care and devotion to patients and not so centred on maximising their incomes, unlike those lesser mortals drawn to Dentistry! The progressive expansion of professorial staff over the next quarter of a century is laid out in the following table and in most departments there was also a concomitant expansion of lecturers.

Professorial Appointments and Retirements

1944	William James Wilson relinquished office of Dean of the Medical Faculty
1944	John Henry Biggart installed as Dean
1945	C.H.G. Macafee succeeded C.G. Lowry to Chair of Midwifery and Gynaecology
1947	Harold William Rodgers succeeded Professor Crymble to Chair of Surgery
1948	Henry Barcroft resigned the Dunville Chair of Physiology on being appointed to the Chair of Physiology at St. Thomas' Hospital Medical School, London
1948	Archibald David Greenfield appointed to Chair of Physiology
1947	Alan C. Stevenson appointed to Chair of Social and Preventive Medicine, replacing former Chair of Public Health, which had been held by W.J. Wilson
1948	Philip Joseph Stoy appointed to new Chair of Dentistry
1948	Frederick M.B. Allen appointed to new Chair of Child Health
1947–8	John Henry Biggart appointed as Director of the Institute of Pathology
1950	W.W.D. Thomson retired from the Chair of Medicine
1950–51	S.B. Boyd Campbell appointed acting Professor of Medicine during vacancy
1952	J.J. Pritchard appointed to Chair of Anatomy
1952	Graham M. Bull appointed to Chair of Medicine
1953–4	J. Small resigned from Chair of Botany
1954–5	George W. Dick appointed to new Chair of Microbiology
1954–5	John G. Gibson appointed to new Chair of Mental Health
1954–5	Owen L. Wade appointed to new Chair of Therapeutics and Pharmacology
1957–8	John Pemberton appointed to Chair of Social and Preventive Medicine following resignation of Alan Stevenson, who moved to Directorship of MRC Human Population Genetics Research Unit, Oxford

1958–9	Richard B. Welbourn appointed to Personal Chair in Surgical Science
1961–2	Eric Cheeseman appointed to Personal Chair in Medical Statistics in Department of Social and Preventive Medicine
1962–3	Retirements of Professors Macafee and Allen
1963	Ivor J. Carré appointed to Chair of Child Health
1964	John W. Dundee appointed to Personal Chair in Anaesthetics
1964	J.H. Scott appointed to Personal Chair in Dental Anatomy
1964	J.H.M. Pinkerton appointed to Chair of Midwifery and Gynaecology
1964	A.D.M. Greenfield resigned from Chair of Physiology to take up similar post in St. Mary's Hospital, London
1964–5	Ian C. Roddie appointed to Chair of Physiology
1965–6	Graham Bull resigned from the Chair of Medicine on appointment to the Directorship of the MRC's Research Centre, Northwick Park, London
1965–6	George Dick resigned Chair of Microbiology to take Chair at Middlesex Hospital, London
1966	John Vallance-Owen appointed to Chair of Medicine
1966	John Dundee appointed to new Chair of Anaesthetics
1966	Kenneth B. Frazer appointed to Chair of Microbiology
1967	John Lloyd appointed to Chair of Biochemistry
1967–8	E. Florence McKeown appointed to Personal Chair in Morbid Anatomy
1967–8	Peter Elmes appointed to Personal Chair in Therapeutics and Pharmacology
1968–9	Peter Froggatt appointed to Personal Chair in Epidemiology in Department of Social and Preventive Medicine
1968	Establishment of new Chair of General Practice (not filled until the appointment of George Irwin in 1971)
1971	Establishment of new Chair of Ophthalmology to be filled in 1972 by Desmond Archer

In 1944 the government-appointed Inter-Departmental Committee on Medical Schools (the Goodenough Committee) put forward its proposals on medical education throughout the United Kingdom. Chairing his first Faculty meeting as Dean, on 19th September 1944, John Henry formed a sub-committee to consider the very significant implications for the Medical School. It reported back to Faculty in April 1946 on expansionary plans to conform to the Goodenough Committee's recommendations; it also, however, incorporated his own visionary ideas for the School. In future the undergraduate curriculum would be extended from five to six years. It was agreed that a new block of buildings would be necessary to house departments of Medicine, Surgery, Midwifery and Gynaecology, Child Health, Therapeutics and Pharmacology, and Ophthalmology, this last-named being represented at the time only by a part-time lectureship. It was accepted that this new building should be built on the Royal Victoria Hospital site on the Grosvenor Road, a mile away from the main University campus.

On 5th July, 1948, in accord with the introduction of the new Health Services Act, the responsibility for the voluntary and local authority hospitals and their equipment was devolved from the Ministry of Health at Stormont to the newly formed Northern Ireland Hospitals' Authority (NIHA). It was initially housed in the Friend's Provident Building, Howard Street, Belfast. The Authority was born precipitously and in many ways found it difficult to understand and assume the many responsibilities that had been passed down to it. Its Secretary, Eric Jones, who had much to do with the comparative success of the NIHA, even admitted this in his first Annual Report:

> Unremitting labour at high pressure overcame the disabilities and disadvantages resulting from lack of adequate preparation before July 1948, but even at the end of the year there were many unresolved problems and doubts about solutions to other problems.

The Authority needed all the help and advice that it could get from those with experience to give it. Among those to whom it turned was John Henry. It was a potential vacuum, tailor-made for him, who could act as the main link and catalyst between the University, the Royal Victoria Hospital Management Committee and the NIHA officials, and use his forceful personality to persuade his colleagues into seeing things his way. Thus, he was quick to recognise that it was the NIHA's statutory duty to co-operate with Queen's University in the local implementation of the Goodenough Committee's recommendations. Immediately, he set about persuading the NIHA, with Ministry of Health approval, to transfer an extensive area of ground adjacent to the Royal Victoria Hospital to Queen's so that new buildings, first mooted in 1946, could be erected to provide better accommodation and facilities for the clinical academic staff.

In January 1948, a Medical Faculty sub-committee, chaired by Professor W.W.D. Thomson, proposed that

> a Directorship of the Institute of Pathology should be established in order to bring closer liaison between the clinical departments and more effective utilisation of teaching facilities available at various hospitals.

It was impressed, also, by the necessity for

> a general Administrator of the Institute to assume responsibility for building alterations, repairs, upkeep of ground and premises and general utility services, organising the teaching facilities, and apportioning rooms to constituent Departments. The Director should endeavour to make the Institute a link between the Pre-clinical Departments of the University and the Clinical Departments in the Hospitals. He should also promote closer co-ordination in teaching and research between the various clinical subjects through the common foundation of Pathology. As an extra he was also to act as chairman of the Heads of Departments in relation to co-ordination of salaries of technicians.

This job description had of course been drafted to fit John Henry like a tailored suit. Faculty chorused its approval of these laudable aims and had no hesitation in throwing yet another mantle over John Henry's shoulders. What a power base he had now! Fulfilment of one of his many dreams was now within his grasp. An extra floor was added to the Institute of Pathology and completed in 1950. Adjacent and opposite this arose the impressive and spacious Institute of Clinical Science incorporating academic department offices, research laboratories, and two large lecture theatres for the clinical medical students. These were officially opened in 1953. Also in the latter building was the Medical Library originally housed on the main University campus. Not everyone in the University was impressed by these developments; they felt that the decentralisation had weakened the mother campus. However, from the Medical School's aspect, the building was a major advance, being a critical factor in the attraction of academic staff of high quality and often of national and international repute. John Henry was acutely aware of the parochial nature of Ulster and the danger of the Medical School falling into mediocrity by confining appointments in clinical subjects to local applicants, as had been almost exclusively the case (though to answer the question of access to hospital beds rather than blatant nepotism), since the Queen's school had opened in 1849. As mentioned above there was a significant expansion in the number of Chairs created and many of these were filled by men of distinction from England, Scotland and Wales as well as further afield such as South Africa and Australia. The interaction of these with the most talented locals formed an impressive formula to put Queen's on the international map.

The importance of 'team spirit' in bonding had been deeply ingrained in John Henry's psyche since his school days on the rugby field. In March 1956 he suggested the establishment of an annual Medical Faculty lunch as a social occasion where Faculty members of all specialties and seniority, and their wives and partners, could meet in a totally relaxed atmosphere. This event was held at Queen's in late May or early June until his retirement in 1971. It created a focal meeting point where new friendships could be forged and newly appointed staff could be assimilated into the team. The ladies were encouraged to turn out in all their finery. At the end of the meal John Henry would make a light-hearted speech ending with his presentation of a verbal award to the lady whom he deemed to be adorned in the most attractive hat. The ladies soon learned to fall in with this custom and vied with each other to be crowned as victrix.

John Henry was also undoubtedly one of the main architects in moulding the format of the so-called *Joint Appointment* system introduced by the University and the NIHA in 1949. The scheme was unique in the United Kingdom and provided that future appointment to Chairs, lectureships and other permanent posts, mainly in the clinical and service laboratory departments, should be made jointly by the University and the NIHA. Each of the employing authorities contributed towards a combined salary for the services undertaken on their behalf. This allowed access of academic staff to the Distinction Award System of the National Health Service and the resultant opportunity to supplement their salaries on merit and so negate the financial advantages of full-time clinical staff who had recourse to private practice for a limited number of sessions, and this could be detrimental to recruitment to the academic ranks of many of the brightest careerists. It must be said that the introduction of the scheme was resented by many of the non-academic NHS consultants who felt that they were being deprived of awards that should otherwise have come their way; but the system on balance served the Medical School well for 45 years and was another all-important factor in attracting national and international staff of distinction. It also must be said that it had no friends among the powers that be in Britain, but the reasons are too complex to debate here. I will just say that of recent years the Joint-Appointment System has come under increasing analysis and criticism from the University Authorities. This has been due to the vast increase in Health Service clinical work and administrative bureaucracy without a concomitant increase in clinical and academic staff numbers. These factors have often, with parasitic fervour, eroded the time available to the Joint Appointees to carry out productive research. As the government has deemed that much of its funding to a university should be dependent on that university's success in attracting outside research funds, a major crisis has developed and the University sector has felt short-changed. The valuable teaching contributions made by joint appointees have been intentionally ignored by a succession of governments, since this fails to raise any significant funds from outside bodies.

John Henry held strongly to the view that teaching held equal sway with research in the contribution of an academic. Some academics were more talented in one than the other. It was also his view that the clinical university staff should be involved in the wards, diagnosing and treating patients; he had little time for the academics who wished to divorce themselves from the practical aspects of clinical medicine by secreting themselves in 'ivory towers'. In Queen's he decided, against the trend of ever-increasing specialisation, to introduce an experimental teaching curriculum based on his view *that there was but one subject to teach – 'that of Medicine', and that there was but one patient – 'the sick patient'.*

In 1950 in an effort to meet the demands and standards of the General Medical Council, he and his colleagues developed a teaching system termed the Combined Clinical Curriculum. In this the Microbiologist, Pathologist, Physician, Surgeon, Sociologist and Therapeutician each looked at the same problem through his or her own particular window. It was hoped in this way to bring it home to the students that all these specialists were attempting to contribute to the individual patient's well-being.

John Henry felt that he wanted to be involved personally in influencing the local improvement, modernisation and expansion of medical facilities throughout Northern Ireland. Perhaps this was one of his weak points: he did not delegate easily. He felt that delegation to another could fail to deliver the package that he could have achieved. He also much preferred to be chairman rather than a mere member, of a committee and once admitted to me that he felt relatively ineffectual when not in the Chair. As a result he found himself on numerous university and hospital committees, frequently as chairman: when not in the Chair his membership tended to be shorter than when he was! He was, for example, Chairman of the Laboratory Services Committee, NIHA, 1948–54, Chairman of the Medical Education and Research Committee, NIHA, 1950–64 and on the Joint Advisory Committee with the Northern Ireland Tuberculosis Authority (NITA), 1955–9, when the latter disbanded, its main job done. Also at various periods he served as a member of the Finance and General Purposes Committee, NIHA and of its Grading and Grading Appeals Committees. His attendance at these meetings involved a tremendous time commitment on top of his intra-university work. Often the Authority meetings extended to eight o'clock before he was able to return home for his evening meal. Nevertheless it was by these means that he remained aware of all that was going on and he could act as an all-important cog in the machine: as a senior colleague once put it 'he didn't always actually like committees, but he liked to know what was going on'.

Even with his seemingly inexhaustible energy, John Henry began to feel the need for some administrative help for the paperwork involved in running the rapidly expanding Medical School. So in November 1946 Faculty agreed that there should be a Dean's office with a Senior Executive Officer to look after the increasing, often routine, office work involving also the enrolment and interviewing of students, whilst referring all matters of weight and principle to him. This post, termed Secretary to the Faculty of Medicine, was held first by an ex-colonial bacteriologist from the West Indies, Dr Peter Clearkin. Dr Stewart Johnston (brother of Dr Wilson Johnston, the Queen's University Student Medical Officer) succeeded him in October 1951. He also had been in the Colonial Service since 1927 and had served in Malaya during the war where he was interned between 1941 and 1945.

These men were an immense help to John Henry. They relieved him of the drudgery of the more tedious tasks and paperwork involved in running the Medical School. Stewart Johnston died in 1956 and since no medically qualified successor could be found it was decided that many of the office and routine duties could be discharged by a young woman who had acted as typist for Peter Clearkin and Stewart Johnston. This was Colleen Kearney (later to become Colleen Jackson) who, although paid a pittance compared to her medically qualified predecessors, ran the Faculty Office with tact and efficiency for the rest of John Henry's working life. She was strong enough to stand up to his forceful character and able to protect him from some of the more awkward and persistent students and staff, who were seeking an audience often on some trivial matter.

John Henry placed a great deal of importance on interviewing prospective medical students. Competition for places on the Faculty roll became extremely keen after the war and the quality of the local applicants remained high. Queen's University, like other Irish medical schools, had always been an exporting one. Only about 30% of the graduates could expect to find employment in Northern Ireland: the rest would scatter to the ends of the earth, or more accurately to the English-speaking parts. John Henry insisted on interviewing all those who had attained minimum standards in their Senior Certificate or, later, the GCE A Levels. He deeply regretted the necessity to demand Advanced levels in Chemistry and Physics. This forced the schools to adopt a programme of specialisation in these two subjects at the early age of fourteen, to the detriment of the broadly based education that he had been able to take in his own school days at Inst. In 1945, with his deep-rooted belief in the educational benefits of the structured languages of the Classics, he had managed to postpone a proposal in Faculty to abolish Latin at Junior Certificate level as a requirement of admission but finally had to succumb reluctantly to the opinions of the day in 1959. His emphasis on the interview was based on his belief that a future doctor needed much more than high examination results. He also came to distrust the glowing references submitted by local Head Teachers who might have gained particular kudos for their small provincial school if one or more of their protégés gained entrance to the Medical School. It was more important to determine that the aspiring candidate had a fundamental kindly and caring outlook towards those suffering in society. An examination swot with no broadly based talents might be rejected as unsuitable. It was rumoured that the candidate's prospects were significantly enhanced should they have short well-groomed hair, played rugby and wore the tie of a well known grammar school in the centre of Belfast. Ladies were obviously at a disadvantage, but only a few initially applied due to the inadequacy (or absence) of Science laboratories (other than Domestic Science) in all-female schools. In spite of the constant pressure from local applicants for the available places, each year he insisted on reserving at least 5% of the intake for students from abroad. He was always trying to break down the parochial outlook of the Ulster folk and knew that it could do nothing but good for the locals to have the opportunity to broaden their views by rubbing shoulders with those emanating from other cultures. So over the years there was always a small nucleus of interesting characters from Africa, USA, Canada, Hungary, Malaysia and Norway, and even from nearby England.

Later in their undergraduate careers, a few students would have to face John Henry across the Medical Faculty desk under very different circumstances. They had either repeatedly failed to satisfy their examiners or had been reported to the Dean for some misdemeanour. The offending students would often be kept waiting outside his office in a state of trembling anticipation. He would then beckon them into his inner sanctum and gruffly read them the riot act on their poor performance, sometimes threatening them with ejection from the Medical School. Very few students, however, suffered this ultimate fate, for, more often than not, John Henry's features would suddenly soften and mischievous twinkles settle in his eyes, before he sent them off for another attempt or with words of warning on their future behaviour. I can comment with some authority on these matters from direct experience. Together with the other student representatives of my undergraduate year, I was summoned to his high court, after participating in a raid on the Nurse's Quarters at the Royal Victoria Hospital following a boisterous Christmas party. Matron Florence Elliott, who also struck fear into all those around her, had interviewed us first before reporting our allegedly dastardly deeds to the Dean. He verbally skinned us alive, before sending us on our way with a wry smile and a pat on our backs, acknowledging that sometimes the intensity of medical studies necessitated the release of 'animal spirits'. Little did I know at the time that our aberrant behaviour paled into insignificance when compared with his own and those of some of his contemporaries in the 1920s.

In the *Belfast Telegraph* of 17th March 1965, an article stated that John Henry

> to his students has always been a crusty figure whose 'bark is worse than his bite'. His enemies in the power struggle (in other Queen's faculties) have suggested that the students have got it the wrong way round.

In 1967, just after the award of his knighthood had been announced, two students were waiting for a disciplinary interview outside his Faculty office. One student was overheard asking the other – 'Do you think it would do us any good, if we offered to polish his armour?'

Conveniently sited on the University Road at the junction with Claremont Street a well-known wine-merchant plied his trade. The shop thrived on the support of local academics, businessmen, teachers and even doctors. Customers were always cheerfully and respectfully greeted by the patron, Johnny Rath, a diminutive moustached figure wearing a flat cap and dwarfed by his full-length apron. His sons, Brendan and Frank, followed him into the trade. Frank had aspired to become a doctor but had to withdraw after having had difficulty with his early professional examinations and quailing at the sight of blood. Most customers purchased their needs at the front counter and went on their way totally unaware that there was more to this establishment than met the eye. Johnny's best customers were led

Drawing of Johnny Rath in his apron and cap (*c.* 1955)

to the back of the shop where a narrow corridor sloped downwards before opening into a small storage room or cellar with whitewashed brick walls. In the depth of winter a large flickering log fire in the wall cosily warmed this Spartan room. Around the fire were scattered a few empty crates, a few rickety kitchen chairs and a solitary large and equally rickety rocking chair. Needless to say John Henry fell into the category of one of the best customers and the large rocking chair seemed reserved for his stocky figure. On his way home, he would regularly drop in to restock his home 'pub', before being ushered down to the little den where he settled himself in the rocking chair with a generous glass of the 'crater' in one hand and his pipe in the other. Here he would relish the chat with the other privileged few, all well-educated men from differing backgrounds. Very few medical men had access though a local practitioner, who lived exactly opposite on University Road, regularly did. No doubt, the problems of the world were discussed and solutions proposed. Jokes, often risqué, were shared. Indeed it was here that John Henry heard most of the jokes that he eventually tried out on his secretaries before incorporating the more acceptable of them in his lectures. On the one occasion that I was privileged to accompany him, it was a bitter winter's day. My father, in his broad brimmed black hat and his sombre black overcoat, seemed to me to bear more than a passing resemblance to a 'Godfather of the Mafia', as he settled in his rocking chair and conversed with the other high ranking members of the cabal.

Chapter 12

Postgraduate medical and dental education

Born into a family of school teachers, John Henry always had a driving desire, and the ability to educate those around him. I have already mentioned his talents in imparting his wealth of medical and worldly knowledge to his students and pathology trainees. His interests, however, did not rest there: he considered it self-evident that a newly qualified young doctor was but on the first rung of a long steep ladder leading to a lifetime of learning in a rapidly changing world of scientific discovery; and, moreover, the balance of emphasis within the profession generally would become more fluid and the curriculum and training programmes would have to accommodate to these dynamics.

Only two years after his return to Belfast as the new Professor of Pathology, he was invited to become President of the Belfast Medical Students' Association. Even at this early stage, (1939) he chose 'Postgraduate Study' as the title of his Presidential Address. As was his wont, he began by quoting his favourite physician-philosopher Sir William Osler – 'If the licence to practice, meant the completion of his education, how sad it would be for the young practitioner, how distressing for his patients'. John Henry emphasised in his lecture the need to be chary of considering the attainment of the magical title of 'Doctor' as an endpoint to study and learning.

When he became Dean of the Faculty of Medicine in 1944, he found that the local Ministry of Health was turning to the University to help to establish and co-ordinate postgraduate refresher courses for those young doctors who were starting to return from wartime service to civilian life. He wholeheartedly supported this initiative and gained the co-operation of his university clinical colleagues in agreeing to arrange appropriate classes for these returnees to help with their reintegration into the community.

It fell also to the Faculty to co-ordinate, and the teaching hospitals to provide, courses for those in general practice as well as courses for those wishing to take the higher qualifications necessary to become hospital specialists (e.g. MRCP, FRCS, etc.). By 1947 he was proposing to concentrate postgraduate teaching and co-ordination on the Belfast City Hospital site even though the appropriate resources of the Royal Victoria Hospital were clearly superior. However, he thought that to centre the entire spectrum of such education at the Royal – with its neighbouring specialist hospitals – would be too centripetal, and by involving the City Hospital he aspired also to encourage and raise the morale of the staff and administration of this former Poor Law Union Infirmary, dating from 1838. He also felt that such a move would leave more room on the Royal Victoria site for development of ever evolving new specialist subjects.

Postgraduate teaching continued unstructured and haphazard through the late 1940s and early 1950s after which, especially from the foundation of the College of General Practitioners on the 19th November 1952, (later the 'Royal College' from 1967, although the actual Royal Charter was not presented by Prince Philip until 1972, when he was President) and parallel moves by the established Royal Colleges (these are too detailed to consider here), the pace quickened, though in retrospect did not quicken enough. In 1962, anticipating recommendations in the Todd Report of 1968 (*Royal Commission on Medical Education, 1965–68*), Faculty nominated Professor Graham Bull (Medicine), Professor John Pemberton (Social Medicine) and John Henry himself to represent it on a Ministry of Health committee to examine the further education and training of general practitioners. Structured post-graduate education now began to take centre stage. This stimulated Faculty to establish a committee of Heads of Departments to explore the needs and provision of Postgraduate Medical Education (or 'Continuing Medical Education' – CME – as it came to be called), with the possibility of framing a coherent scheme suitable for an application to the Nuffield Trust. By 1963 the Dean was informing Faculty that both Altnagelvin (Londonderry) and Belfast City Hospital were eager to participate in the scheme for CME for GPs. Owing to the amount of extra work entailed Faculty agreed to investigate the feasibility of creating a new post of Dean of Postgraduate Studies ('Postgraduate Dean'), although it must be admitted that John Henry was reluctant to share the name 'Dean' with anyone. Within a few months the University had authorised the appointment of part-time clinical tutors, at an honorarium not exceeding £150 p.a. each; also clinical lecturers at the rate of £4-4-0 per half-day session. The Ministry was soon to provide some £55,000 (£1,000 p.a.) for the development of Postgraduate Education in Northern Ireland: at last the pace was quickening.

In January 1964 Faculty established a Postgraduate Medical Board comprising representatives from the Faculty, the Northern Ireland Hospitals Authority, the Northern Ireland General Health Services Board, the BMA, the Department of Public Health, the College of General Practitioners and the Ministry. Its main remit was to consider (a) the development of GP refresher courses and (b) specialist training of junior hospital medical staff. John Henry also suggested that the Board should submit a scheme to the Nuffield Trust, proposing the establishment of medical libraries in large provincial hospitals. By September it was agreed that the post of Director of Postgraduate Studies (not 'Dean' be it noted!) should be advertised (this post, surprisingly, had first been mooted by the Ministry as early as 1943 but after being kicked from pillar to post between the University, Ministry and the Goodenough Committee, it eventually floundered for 22 years amidst the complexities of reorganising the Health Service).

There were four applicants leading to the appointment in June 1965 of Dr John McKnight, a highly focused and respected Belfast general practitioner. Eventually the Postgraduate Council for Medical and Dental Education emerged and in 1969 John Henry, who was due to retire from the Medical Faculty Deanship and Chair of Pathology in 1971, was appointed its Chairman. John McKnight and my father, both men of vision, worked harmoniously together; John McKnight took the lead role and had the energy to carry his definite but sound ideas forward; John Henry, on the other hand, had the experience and wide influential contacts to make the finance and ideas materialise. They formed a great team and, with Dr George Irwin appointed a foundation Professor of General Practice in October 1971, the fourth such chair in the UK, and with the hospital academic and clinical staff supportive, standards of postgraduate medical training throughout Northern Ireland came to be the envy of many of the other UK centres. John Henry remained in this role until succeeded by Professor D.A.D. (Desmond) Montgomery in early 1979; as it transpired only months before my father died suddenly in London on GMC business.

My father rose energetically to the challenge of the advent and progress of structural postgraduate education, and with a clear insight of what was required and at what pace and to what depths the profession would accept. Unquestionably, his philosophy, his practical acumen, and his strong grasp of the dynamics of what would be involved; his position in crucial strategic points in medical educational and practice development through his membership of the GMC and most influential medico-educational bodies in Ulster; and his position in central and even in more peripheral yet relevant, planning and administrative positions for a whole legislative area (Northern Ireland), not just helped but allowed him effectively to influence strongly, even control, the necessary steps to be taken in response. He retired from the University before the impact of the Todd report was translated into curricular changes, and similarly those resulting from the 1978 Medical Act, but he had foreseen, and agreed with, many of them, and had laid the groundwork for his successors.

Chapter 13

Home life and summer holidays

On return to Belfast from Edinburgh in 1937 the family took up residence in No. 2 Malone Park, a prestigious private tree-lined avenue, separated from the general public on the main Lisburn Road thoroughfare by impressive pillars and gates. My memories of this period are scanty as I lived here only until I was four. I remember rather dark, spacious and poorly carpeted rooms shaded by tall trees. There was a patch of rising damp and peeling wallpaper on the kitchen wall that was a cause of concern to my mother. Two white recumbent stone lions guarded the entrance. Professor Henry Barcroft, son of the distinguished Cambridge physiologist, Sir Joseph Barcroft, and who would himself become equally so and who at that time held the Dunville Chair of Physiology at Queen's University, lived two further doors up and I remember playing with his son, Jeremy, and contracting a severe dose of whooping cough from him. My final recollection of this period is of the elopement of our redheaded Scottish maid complete with boyfriend and my mother's gold watch.

In 1940 my father noticed a large house for rent, at the other side of town in the east of the city. It had the potential to fulfill his childhood dreams of living graciously. Thus Creevlea, 64 King's Road, became the Biggart home, rented until 1944, then purchased for £4,000 and not sold until my mother was forced by ill-health to enter a residential home in 1990. It had three spacious reception rooms with high ceilings, picture rails and draughty bay windows. The drawing room was bright and sunny having a southerly and westerly aspect overlooking the floral gardens. In contrast the dining room and study tended to be rather dark as the tall trees cast their shadows. From a gloomy hall, the staircase and its highly polished mahogany bannister rose, first to a cold white-tiled bathroom and the adjacent 'half-way house', before climbing further to the landing and five bedrooms, all but one with unused open fire-places, and further up still to the attic. From the hall three steps

John Henry's family house, 64 King's Road, Knock, Belfast

descended to the kitchen quarters where, off a short understair corridor lay the cloakroom and beside this a chilly pantry which was soon to be christened 'THE PUB'. It was here that John Henry was to store the wines and spirits that were often to fire his soul.

The kitchen was home for a massive black metal cooking range and a wooden 'Sheila' for drying clothes, suspended on pulleys from the 12 foot-high ceiling. Next came the scullery where the dishes were washed by hand and the pastry rolled for meat pies and apple tarts. Another little pantry contained 'the sieve', a free-standing cupboard measuring about three feet in all dimensions with its door and side walls separated from the surrounding air by finely perforated metal mesh which served to ward off the abundant bluebottles and wasps from the meat, butter, jams and other delicacies, and to keep the food fresh for as long as possible. It was the precursor of the modern refrigerator. The kitchen quarters rambled to their conclusion in the washhouse with its coarsely tiled floor and twin 'jaw boxes' (deep porcelain sinks) in which the clothes were hand-washed using a huge block of soap and a washboard. The sodden clothes were then passed through the rollers of the 'ringer', or mangle, to squeeze out as much water as possible. Beneath the shelves, eggs were preserved under waterglass in clay crocks resembling large flowerpots.

The above were the basic ingredients of the house which my parents slowly transformed into their own little 'Victorian palace' and a home full of happiness. In many ways John Henry adhered to old-fashioned values of style and etiquette. Regency striped wallpaper appeared in the hall and was very effective. The drawing-room walls became crowded with watercolour paintings, mostly within ornate gold frames. Among these was a magnificent depiction by Samuel Prout of the intricacies of the altar-screen in Chartres Cathedral. This held pride of place above the mantelpiece. Others included Venetian canal scenes by Skinner Prout, a tranquil river vista by Egginton, a scribe in North Africa writing a letter accompanied by a kneeling lady in purdah by David Roberts, a stormy Donegal landscape by Frank McKelvey, and a picture of three sporting nymphs in a field whose creator I have forgotten. I christened the last as 'The Three Bare Ladies' and this stuck in family parlance. There was much discussion as to whether the left thigh of one of the nymphs was truly in proportion.

My father, on his retirement, had time to gather together all his academic medals for display within a small gold frame above the bureau. Unfortunately, these were stolen a few years later when the house was burgled by youngsters, who opened and sampled a few bottles of whiskey and brandy in the 'pub', but obviously, disliking the taste, left the almost full bottles for finger-printing, by the police. On realising that the medals were of no tangible value to them, they smashed the covering glass and threw the medals into a garden of a house no more than a hundred yards further down King's Road. From there the majority of the medals were duly returned by a neighbour, but several were never recovered.

After my father's death I was astonished to discover that all the works of art in the house were insured for only £300. In addition to the more standard settee and armchairs, a William IV expandable table sat by the window and a Victorian roll-top writing bureau and china cabinet occupied the available wall space. Above the cabinet sat a painted china plate clock with unusual scrolled edges. Chelsea and Beau figurines kept it company. Through the cabinet's glass doors could be seen a horde of treasures – a superb collection of Waterford cut-glass, gold rimmed Royal Doulton dinner sets and Royal Worcester plates with individually hand-painted scenes and some brightly coloured Bavarian glassware. Elsewhere in the room every available shelf was home for Royal Doulton and, in later years, Capodimonte figurines. Further landscape paintings of the Dutch Masters' school adorned the dining room walls and complemented the Adam-style grey and white marble fireplace. There were also some cheap prints such as 'The Laughing Cavalier' by Frans Hals and 'Girl reading letter at Open Window' by Jan Vermeer van Delft. Book shelves and a magnificent early Victorian mahogany desk with inlaid green leatherwork and multiple drawers dominated the study.

As the years passed a certain amount of modernisation was undertaken, but this was minimal. Shelves in the study were extended to reach ever higher towards the ceiling to accommodate John Henry's avid appetite for literature. The range in the kitchen was removed and replaced by an open fire with a back boiler, so converting it into a cosy living room for the housekeeper and her visiting friends. The cooking thereafter was on a gas cooker in the scullery. Elsewhere Victoriana (or was it Sparta?) ruled. There was not and there never was to be the installation of central heating: John Henry did not like it and thought it unhealthy – so that was that. My mother was also brought up believing in the beneficial effects of fresh air, so even on the frostiest of nights the bedroom windows were left six inches open. These factors plus the ill-fitting draughty sash windows provided an airy existence.

One of the major benefits of life in such a house was the requirement of employing a servant. In 1940 my mother interviewed several applicants for the post of live-in maid and duly appointed a petite girl called Mary McGuire. I remember that she wore a uniform comprising a black dress with a frilly white apron and a little tiara-shaped white cap of similar material. Her skill at ironing was a wonder to behold and my father was particularly pleased with her laundering of his white shirts with their starched cuffs and separate collars. She stayed for a few years before moving on. Thereafter there was a succession of unsatisfactory replacements, one of whom was sacked on the spot after my parents returned unexpectedly early from an engagement to discover her in bed with an American soldier. Then came Sadie McCrory who arrived as a young girl of nineteen and remained with the family for thirty years and then left only because her mother was

WAY BACK FROM THE ROAD

Let me live for a time way back from the road
Where very few folks go by
With some books, a few friends, and a woodland trail
And above me a clear blue sky
I'm willing to work all the days of the week
And most of the hours each day
But I do want a house way back from the road
Where I sometimes can get away.

Let me see from my house way back from the road
Bright flowers and a bird that sings
Where no one can tell me of grief and pain
And a telephone never rings
I would turn not away from the sorrows and aches
That seem to be part of my life
If at times I could get away back from the road
And escape for a time the strife.

There are times when I must get me back from the road
And permit mankind to go by:
It suffers, it sorrows:
With its grief, with its pain –
Shared in it all have I.
I seem a part of the grief of the world
With myriads of men.
So at times I must rest me way back from the road
Then share it all over again.

My sister came into the world in 1942 and was six years my junior; it took my mother that length of time to recover from the agony and prolonged labour of my birth. Indeed she had earlier sworn that her family was complete but she finally decided on another child as a defiant act to thwart Hitler.

For most of the time my sister and I, as young children, saw my father only before bedtime on weekdays and at the weekends. Our discipline was almost entirely in the hands of our mother who became more than efficient in delivering a sharp slap to the back of our bare legs, when we stretched her patience to the limit. Thereupon my mother's usual calm and cheerful demeanour would suddenly desert her and she would be transformed into a raging red-faced dervish whacking everyone in her path whether deserving or not. Sometimes this led to one or other of us feeling a sense of injustice. Then the storm would subside as quickly as it arose and we were all left engulfed in remorse.

I remember one such episode just after the war in 1947 when my parents travelled by boat and train to attend a medical conference in Switzerland. In the belief that the War had deprived us of many of the joys of childhood, my parents struggled back with an exotic doll for Rosemary, a six feet high kite for both of us that we never got into the air, and a brightly coloured wooden gun for me. The latter had a compression mechanism that fired arrows with rubber-suction ends at a numbered metal target. I was thrilled with the gun, but once I had become fairly proficient at hitting the bull's eye I thought that it would be much more fun to seek out a live target and my four-year old sister's forehead seemed ideal. Just as I was taking aim, the gun was snatched from my grasp by my irate mother, who broke it over her knee and threw it on the coal fire – an injustice that still rankles, as I never would have fired. I was really just pretending! My mother got all the blame for being so fiery in such matters, whilst our father, who was so rarely there, got all the credit for being so much more understanding, tolerant and fair. Only on one occasion did he become so exasperated as to lift his hand to me. He was teaching me as a five-year-old child to play tiddlywinks and allowed me to win the first three games, before soundly trouncing me in the fourth. I thought that I should win every game and burst into tears. I was quickly put across his knee and given something to cry for as his hand descended several times with force on my backside and he gave me an indelible lecture on being a good loser. I have hopefully been a good sport ever since.

At a later stage in life I was again the recipient of his extreme tolerance. I had just turned seventeen and was impatient to master the art of driving. My father owned a black Triumph Renown with its characteristic straight-edged and box-like outlines with its instantly identifiable registration mark – OZ 194. So on occasions, he moved over into the passenger seat and endured many scary moments as his son pressed on the accelerator rather than the brake or made some other elementary error. One very cold December he had to travel to a General Medical Council Meeting in London and asked me to warm up the car's engine in the garage each day of his absence. Anti-freeze was not yet in vogue and starting a cold obstinate engine could necessitate cranking it with a metal handle inserted through the radiator grille. Such activity in the past had resulted in a lot of huffing and puffing and a ruddy John Henry becoming ruddier, and sometimes ending up with a severely bruised hand as the handle could recoil viciously. I was delighted to seize the chance to get behind the wheel and enhance my newly learned skills; but not content to warm the engine by letting it idle in neutral gear in the garage, I put it into reverse and slowly backed into the pitch-blackness of the winter evening. I turned the wheel as I moved in the familiar arc that would take me past the study bay window to the front of the house, *or so I thought*. The car gave a sudden jolt and juddered to a stop. Gripped with apprehension I got out and found that I had steered much too sharp an arc and had ended up with the back wheels in a flowerbed with the back bumper overlying a short tree stump. No obvious damage to the bodywork. Large sigh of relief. Get that car back into the garage quick. Into first gear, gently does it. The back wheels whirred. The car wouldn't budge. By now in a cold sweat I reinvestigated the problem. The wheels had spun in the damp soil and the stump had now passed upwards between the chassis and the substantial bumper, totally impaling the car. I was left with no alternative but to wait in fear and trepidation for the wrath of my father on his return two days later. White faced I approached him and stammered out my story. Much to my amazement he gave only a quiet grunt and patted me on the back saying 'Och, don't worry, son, we all have to learn.' Never did I appreciate his patience and kindness so much. It took a mobile crane to lift the car from its partial burial.

In our early childhood, on a typical day my father would arrive home about 7.15 p.m. after work in time to discuss what we had learned at school that day and to read us a bedtime story before we were packed off to bed to ensure twelve hours of healthy sleep. He would then settle down in his favourite armchair by the fireside and would have a sherry or two with my mother whilst they caught up with the day's events and browsed over the current news in the *Belfast Telegraph*. About 8 p.m. the bell by the fireplace would be pressed as a signal to the housekeeper to serve dinner in the dining room. After dinner he would often have a snooze for half an hour before awakening refreshed to reach for the most recent medical journals by which he kept up to date with medical advances. He had a remarkably retentive memory that outshone those of his fellow pathologists and many of the clinicians. From this pool of medical literature he would glean ideas for research topics to offer as suggestions to his trainee pathology staff. Sometimes late in the evening he would prepare for formal lectures to various groups such as the Ulster Medical

Society (e.g. 'Parergon'* (work that is done over and above the daily round), 'Cnidos v Cos'**), or a Presidential address to the Belfast Medical Students Association on 'Postgraduate Education', or to the physiotherapists ('The Future of Disease'***) or perhaps for a school prize day. All and sundry were constantly seeking him as a speaker and rarely, if ever, did he refuse. He prided himself as being an impromptu 'off the cuff' after-dinner speaker and he certainly did not use notes, but again the theme for the speech had usually been devised and stored in his brain late on the previous night.

At other times he had to wade through piles of General Medical Council documentation before attending its meetings in London. His final hour, before retiring to bed often at one or two o'clock, he called 'his schizophrenic hour'. During this, he would become totally introverted and either lose himself in some political biography, or lapse into composing poetry, or in his last decade recall and write down the notable influences on his life. In this reverie a large, but well-diluted tumbler of Black Bush whiskey and frequent puffs on his briar or meerschaum pipe assisted him. My mother accepted this pattern of behaviour with total tolerance. She was content to share the early evening with him conversing on family matters and then to sit quietly listening to the radio or watching television in his company, making only the rare interjection to inquire whether he was comfortable or needed anything. She provided him with the support and the peace and quiet that he so badly required to recharge his batteries. At about eleven o'clock she would bid him a gentle 'goodnight' and leave him to it.

If an item of outside news or a sound penetrated this trance-like hour, it often triggered him to respond in verse or essay. Examples of these reveries included poems entitled 'Atomic Death', stimulated by the dropping of the first Atomic bomb, and a particularly poignant one, reacting to a nearby bomb explosion in our local troubles, entitled 'Belfast 1972'. His emotions were racked with pain as the country he so loved and served, was ripped apart by intercommunity strife. Once, he heard on the local TV news of the separation through violent death of a local pair of completely innocent lovers. The young girl mourning the loss of her boyfriend touched his heartstrings, when she described how she and her murdered lover had gone for quiet walks in the local countryside and enjoyed themselves in their 'Own

*   Biggart, J.H: 'Parergon', *Ulster Medical Journal*, 1949; vol. 18 (2): pp116–28.
** Biggart, J.H.: 'Cnidos v Cos', *Ulster Medical Journal*, 1971; vol. 41 (1): pp 1–9.
*** Biggart, J.H.: 'The Future of Disease', *Physiotherapy*, 1964; pp 355–9.

Wee Way'. John Henry immediately poured out an essay on how the word 'wee' in Ulster meant so much more than 'little'. He ended: 'Yet they had to scale no heights to find their happiness, for curiously in this so turbulent Ulster they had already found it *in their own wee way*. Our prayers are with her, but our tears are for ourselves'.

The above examples hopefully provide the reader with an insight into John Henry's complex character that lay deeply hidden from his professional colleagues, friends and even family. He was a deeply emotional man and at times displayed a slightly melancholic streak.

It was at weekends and holiday breaks that we saw him in relaxed mood. He would on Saturday and Sunday steal a few extra hours in bed. On Saturday he would go into the laboratory about eleven o'clock and tidy up any outstanding items of work before crossing Grosvenor Road to a newsagent shop (Morris's), where he purchased cigarettes, pipe tobacco and a large variety of sweets and chocolate for the family's consumption during the subsequent week. The amalgam fillings in Rosemary's and my teeth now bear witness to his generosity. On one such occasion during the war he returned to the lab to fetch some black market country butter which was stored in the cold room (4°C) alongside the pints of donated blood. He entered the cold room, only to hear the heavy door close with a click behind him as the exterior metal bar fell into its notch. Nowadays, Health and Safety regulations would insist on such a room having a telephone to raise the alarm in such circumstances, but no such phone existed and all the other staff had gone home so there was nobody to hear his muffled shouts through the thick door. There was every possibility that John Henry would have been discovered frozen stiff on Monday as 'the Ulster Ice Man'. Fortunately he retained his composure and eventually managed to squeeze a folded copy of *The Illustrated London News* between the ill-fitting door and its frame to raise the exterior lever and escape. He arrived home about 4 o'clock to be greeted by a distraught wife.

Sundays at home could at times be interesting. My mother was an ardent churchgoer and donned her 'Sunday best' outfit complete with 'Paris model' hat before wending her way down to Knock Presbyterian Church accompanied by her more reluctant children who also had to attend Sunday school in the afternoon.

My father only turned out on Christmas Day and Easter Sunday. I think he felt that he had had enough religion as a child to last him a lifetime. He usually had a long lie-in and would descend to the drawing room in his pyjamas and dressing gown to linger over a leisurely breakfast of buttered farls of toasted soda bread and tea. One Sunday a ring at the front door disturbed him. The housekeeper must have been out at chapel, so he opened it himself to discover two spruce young Americans on the doorstep. They were, of course, Mormons on a mission to save sinners. My father welcomed them into the house before luring them into an in-depth discussion on the pros and cons of all the world religions, about which he was extremely well versed. The young missionaries tried their best to make their case but were completely outgunned. My father finally ushered them out giving them a stern lecture on their audacity at calling on Sunday morning when all good Christian folk would be at their place of worship and only the spiritually weak would be at home.

In *Who's Who* John Henry listed his recreations as reading, writing, music and gardening. Whilst the first three are undoubtedly true, I do not think that he could accurately be described as a gardener, although he loved to relax with the beauty of the garden around him. He would occasionally become despondent about the rate of weed growth in the flowerbeds and do a wee scuffle with the hoe between the roses before raking the weeds into little heaps at the edge of the bed. There they remained as blots on the landscape, often for several days until the gardener or available offspring tidied up after him. He did, however, love flowers and would often spend a summer Saturday afternoon creating artistic arrangements in cut-glass vases for drawing-room décor. One autumn he bought about one thousand tulip bulbs and guided the gardener as to where to plant them for mass effect. Spring came and to his delight the tulips duly painted the multicoloured picture that he had envisaged. The following day the garden was ravaged by a fierce storm causing many of the heavy-headed tulips to snap off from their brittle stems. When my father returned from work that evening he went straight out into the garden returning to the house tenderly cradling in his arms about a hundred beheaded tulips and quite obviously emotionally upset.

Sunday night was music night. Beneath a curtained window-seat in the bay window lay an immense collection of the old 78s and long play records. These extended over a wide spectrum of music and included the symphonies of Beethoven, Brahms and Sibelius as well as the '1812 Overture' by Tchaikovsky and Mozart's four 'Horn Concertos'. There were also the ballads sung by the tenors Count John McCormick, James Johnston, Joseph

Locke and Peter Pears, and the deeper notes of Peter Dawson and Paul Robeson and the contralto, Kathleen Ferrier. Church choirs were a favourite, particularly that of King's College, Cambridge. For some light relief there were a few comic records, one of which was by Jimmy O'Dea, a famous Irish comedian. It was called 'Hands across the Border' and included such expressions as 'Put that in your pipe and smoke it.' and 'Put that in your big drum and beat it.' John Henry expected the entire family to share in his concert and admire these classical gems. Rosemary and I would not hurt him for the world and pretended to be equally entranced, when in fact we felt that we were enduring a form of prolonged torture often lasting for three hours or more. Now that I am older I have come to appreciate and derive great pleasure from classical music and owe yet another debt to my father for introducing me to it, but at that time I would have preferred to listen to Frankie Lane's 'Walking My Baby Back Home.'

On one such evening after the war we were visited by my father's brother, Hugh, and his wife Peggie – an excuse to pour a few gins and tonics (Oh dear! and on a Presbyterian Sunday too). Hugh could in no way be described as a music fan, but my father was not going to forgo his musical session for the sake of his very much younger brother who had to sit back and take his medicine. As the evening wore on and the gin began to affect the audience, a young chorister began to warble, in his treble voice, a song entitled 'The wavy corn'. On and on, over and over again he sang the words 'wavy corn, w-a-v-y c-o-r-n, w—a—v—y c—o—r—n', till Hugh in exasperation abruptly interrupted: 'I wish that bloody farmer would get a move on, cut that corn and plant that field with potatoes!' Everyone, including John Henry roared with laughter.

Hugh had after graduation at Queen's joined the Royal Army Medical Corps, serving in France and Germany until the end of the war by which time he had attained the rank of major, (although later in life he was promoted to colonel). He then specialised in surgery at the Royal Victoria Hospital before becoming an ENT surgeon in the Lurgan and Banbridge areas. He then moved to the new Craigavon Hospital when it opened in 1972. He was his own man and hardened by his experiences he was one of the few prepared to stand up to his elder brother. One Christmas in the mid-1950s Hugh trod on another pet corn. Peggie and Hugh were invited to join the rest of the Biggart clan for Christmas Dinner. John Henry, as we know, was a stickler for upholding the traditions of the past and expected everyone to dress up for the occasion – men in dinner suits and ladies in flowing evening dresses. Hugh, who was twelve years younger and could never be described as a conformist, arrived in a green blazer and worsted grey flannels. This induced a distinct frostiness in the host's welcome but it soon melted as the festive wines flowed. The Christmas feast was eaten in Stygian gloom broken only by the flickering glow of six ornamental candles which lit up the faces of the revellers but hid the offending garments from sight. After the extended family had supped Granny's potato soup and gluttonously devoured the heavy-laden plates of turkey, Brussels sprouts and roast potatoes, it became time for the traditional entry of the Christmas pudding. John Henry retired to the kitchen quarters where he applied a generous dash of brandy to the holly-crowned pudding before striking a match to set it alight. As the ethereal blue flame danced, John Henry proceeded ever so slowly from the kitchen towards the expectant diners. Just as he reached the dining room door a disappointed grunt was heard as the flame gave up its struggle to survive. Down to the kitchen again he went, where he repeated the entire ritual but this time, to be sure to be sure, he soused 'the pud' with almost half a bottle of Courvoisier before rekindling the flame. Triumphant with his belated success he bore the pudding *flambé* to the table, although it was arguable whether the pudding or the ruddy glow of John Henry's cheeks gave off more light.

Social occasions at King's Road were fairly rare, as their preparation tended to cause both my mother and Sadie, the housekeeper, to get into a tizzy. However the occasional dinner party was held and these tended to be fairly formal evenings attended by university professors and medical consultants. Once during the war, the Vice-Chancellor of Queen's, David (later Sir David) Lindsay Keir and his wife were among the guests. The group was ushered into the dining room and took their seats. The other guests were a little overawed at the presence of the V.C. and conversation was at first a little stilted. Lindsay Keir mentioned that he was soon to travel to South America on an official University visit. My mother, trying to maintain the conversational flow and knowing some medical expressions but nothing at all of their meaning, inquired 'Will you have to have your W.R. done?' (For non-medical readers the W.R. test is the Wassermann Reaction which reveals whether a person has been exposed to syphilis). This led, to my mother's complete bewilderment, to an outburst of raucous laughter. The atmosphere immediately relaxed and thereafter went with a swing.

My father naturally exerted control over his children's education and my mother had little influence in this sphere. There was no question about it, even though Campbell College lay conveniently only half a mile from our home, but that I was going to Inst. For the early preparatory years I attended nearby Strathearn School which at that time admitted boys as well as girls into its lower forms. However, from the age of eight I was ferried across town by car across the old Hill Foot Road to Inchmarlo, the Preparatory School of Inst, in Osborne Gardens in the Malone area. This was indeed a duty of love by my father who was not good at getting up in the mornings, and although I was often in trepidation of being late, he always seemed to get me there before the second bell had rung at nine. In the car he was usually very quiet, quelling his smoker's cough with one cheroot after another (it was later in the morning that he switched to his favourite pipe).

Thereafter he took a keen interest in my educational progress, but he discussed my school reports and sporting achievements in a gentle encouraging way and with none of the frightening severity that he had endured from his own father. Nevertheless he held very strong views as to what constituted a proper education. The government of that day had decided that specialisation should take place after the multi-subject Junior Certificate had been taken at the age of fourteen. One was expected then to drop several subjects and concentrate on either the Arts or the Sciences. My father disagreed. He believed, on my behalf, that a general education should be maintained for as long as possible. He thereupon made an appointment with John Grummitt, the Principal of Inst, and successfully persuaded him that I should continue to study Greek, Latin, Ancient History and French at Advanced Level in Senior Certificate and that I could then attend 5th and 6th form classes in Physics and Chemistry during my Upper 6th year. This I successfully accomplished and so received a wider advanced education than most of my contemporaries, but not without difficulties, particularly in the Upper 6th year when I was sometimes tackling problems based on knowledge not yet covered in the 5th form. In retrospect I have no regrets and feel that I have benefited throughout life from the broad spectrum of knowledge. At that time I felt otherwise and at times overburdened.

Rosemary or 'Rosebud', my sister, also felt the influence of father on her education. After attending Strathearn School at Belmont he offered her the opportunity of owning a horse or attending a good boarding school to further her education. Much to her mother's chagrin, she chose the latter.

So it came about that Rosemary at the age of thirteen gained entrance to the famous St Leonard's School in St Andrews, Scotland. There she spent four happy educational years, developing her sporting talents and a streak of independence, which might otherwise have struggled to surface. Each time she returned at the end of term the fatted calf or equivalent was produced; when it was time to return to Scotland buckets of tears were shed by Rosemary and her mother as they clasped each other on the quayside of the Glasgow boat, undoubtedly raising the level of the North Channel by at least an inch.

Often throughout life, Rosemary and I have been asked whether John Henry forced us to take up medicine. The truthful answer is that he did not. If we had opted for another career I do not think that he would have stood in our way. However, perhaps unknowingly, he wove a more subtle spell. Each day we could observe our father totally engulfed by all aspects of his career. He lived and breathed medicine and seemed so fulfilled with his achievements through hard work. Surely no other profession could yield such satisfaction. What option had we? We chose medicine. He was very proud.

* * * * * * * * * * *

In the spring of 1967 the postman delivered a large official cream envelope embossed 'OHMS'. It must have been a Saturday since my father was still enjoying his extra hour in bed. My mother rushed up the stairs in a flap shouting 'Harry, Harry, I hope this isn't what I think it is?' but it was! It was the announcement that John Henry was to be awarded a knighthood in the Queen's Birthday Honours for his longstanding services to medicine. The ceremony was held in Buckingham Palace in July and my mother and sister attended as guests. Thereafter my mother never really came to terms being called 'Lady'; she preferred still to be addressed simply as 'Mrs Biggart' when dealing with shopkeepers and acquaintances. Only when she was forced by ill-health to enter a nursing home in 1990, eleven years after my father's death did she find her title useful. In the informal atmosphere of current times, the nurses wanted to call her by her Christian name, Isobel, but my mother was having none of it. Frail though she was, she put her foot down and compromised (only slightly) to being referred to as 'Lady B'. This they did until her death on 11th August 1996.

John Henry with Isobel and Rosemary after receiving his
Knighthood from the Queen, at Buckingham Palace (1967)

Summer Holidays

Each year John Henry took the entire month of August for his family
holiday. There was never any question of varying the destination – he would
as usual respond to the call of his endemic love of North Antrim and drive
the heavily laden car to the scenic seaside resort of Ballycastle. The journey
took a tedious two-and-a half hours as he sedately drove along the narrow
roads at a steady 40 mph, only accelerating when another more adventurous
driver threatened to pass. To be fair, the roads were at that time not designed
for speed and they provided a far from level surface as they traversed the
unstable foundations of the peat bogs, where the recently cut turfs lay drying

John Henry and daughter dressed for 'Parent and Children's
Tennis Tournament' in Ballycastle, County Antrim (1950)

in neat piles by the roadside. Further north the pungent stench of flax retting
in the ditches would suddenly pervade the car interior and herald to the
impatient children that the marathon was nearing its end.

The family, complete with housekeeper, rented a house towards the lower
part of Quay Hill, a long steep climb that winds upwards from the seafront.
It overlooked the bay and provided panoramic views of the seashore and the
famous rugged headland, Fair Head. This was the base where John Henry
could leave behind his toils and tribulations. Here he could relax completely.
Gone were the heavy biographies and historical treatises that he read at
home. Not even a copy of the *BMJ* or the *Lancet* passed through the

letterbox. In their place he would select half a dozen 'light' mystery novels from the local library and browse over these when the weather was inclement for outside activities.

Holidays at local resorts were usual in those days. The days of sunny continental journeys were not yet in vogue. As a result the same families arrived year after year. There was the 'July group' and the 'August group'. This led to the creation of many friendships and added greatly to the enjoyment. All the locals came to know the regular visitors and the atmosphere (if not always the weather) was warm and welcoming.

John Henry was a creature of habit and each day tended to follow the same ritual. Every morning after a late breakfast he and my mother would stroll up the town to buy the morning newspaper in Kate McLister's, meeting and greeting many familiar faces on the way. They would then move next door for a leisurely coffee in McCollums' Café. On shopping days or if the weather was inclement they went by car. Then back to the house for a scan of the morning paper before it was time to join their close friends, Robin and Dorothy Semple, for a merry-making pre-lunch drink in Paddy McKillop's pub at the sea front. Robin was the Director of Extramural Studies at Queen's University and had a wicked sense of humour. To the frustration of the housekeeper who had prepared lunch, it was often 2.30 p.m. before they returned from their revels in jovial mood and with enhanced complexions.

As my sister and I grew older we spent a great deal of time on the wonderful tennis courts situated at Ballycastle seafront. The grass courts had the unique quality of being playable within half an hour of a heavy shower of rain as they were built on a deep sandy base, which allowed rapid drainage. During the second week of August there was an adult handicap tournament organised for the holidaymakers. My father and mother would participate as a team in the mixed doubles, whilst Robin Semple and John Henry formed a formidable if unfit pair in the men's doubles. It was the latter pairing that caused much entertainment as they often succeeded, with the help of a generous handicap, in scrambling through a few rounds against younger and more orthodox players. In those days it was compulsory for participants to wear white. My father would wear shorts with knee-length socks, whilst Robin Semple was bedecked in longs. They were infamous for their cunning and 'dirty play' as between them they were quite incapable of hitting a straight shot. Both had unorthodox services. John Henry stood sideways to the service line, swung both arms in parallel several times before imparting vicious sidespin to the ball which made it swing away from the receiver whilst rising only a few inches above the receptive grass surface. Robin's service, in contrast, involved equally devastating topspin, which made the ball kick high and in the opposite direction. They complemented each other beautifully as they chopped and lobbed and drop-shotted. On a good day when they were sufficiently accurate they were almost unplayable, at least for one set whilst their puff lasted. I still remember their ecstatic delight when they succeeded in conquering in the first round two much younger acquaintances, Brian Lowry, a medical student at Queen's, and Henry Charlesworth, son of the Professor of Geology.

Towards the end of the month a refreshed John Henry began once more to hear the call of medicine. He made the journey back to Belfast alone. It was time to review the examination results and to select the applicants to the Medical School for the coming year. In his later years as Dean he always insisted on arranging personal interviews for those who had attained the necessary high grades. He earnestly believed that something more than good examination results was necessary to become a doctor. He looked for all-rounded characters who had a deep rooted desire to help their fellowmen at times when they were made vulnerable by ill health. It was recognised, however, that it did not do the candidate any harm at all to wear an Inst School tie or to have played rugby for his school.

Back to Ballycastle he went for the final days of August, which included the famous Auld Llamas Fair, held on the last Tuesday. Of recent years the Fair has been extended to involve the entire week. And then it was *en famille*, back to Belfast.

Chapter 14

Political interlude

My father, unlike some of his colleagues, was little interested in local or national politics and certainly not in being involved in them. He was unquestionably a skilful exponent of what is often referred to as 'political' skills and was imbued with many of the qualities of the true statesman, but he confined the exercise of these to the sphere which he inhabited, that of and associated with his work. At civil elections he was content to follow his unionist family background and traditions, of which he was proud, but he brought up his own family to respect people according to their character and not to their creed or political beliefs, known or presumed, still less to their occupation or position in society. He disliked bigotry in all its forms and from any quarter, and although he adhered to the Presbyterianism of his forebears and insisted, for as long as he could, that his children did likewise including regular church attendance, he himself rarely attended. (I attempted on one occasion to persuade him to throw his weight behind the newly formed Alliance Party (1970), because as I saw it, the inbred intolerance of the Unionist and Nationalist parties was going to perpetuate the instability of Northern Ireland for ever. Supporting the Alliance Party seemed to me to offer a glimmer of hope of forging a means whereby society might at last pull together for the common good of the Province. Perhaps I was naive, but I felt so strongly about this that I agreed to be one of the two hundred signatories who launched the party. My father listened, but I regret that my arguments fell on stony ground and failed to make him budge from his life-long family traditions at this late stage of his life). How and why, then, did this man in a crucial period for Northern Ireland, become involved for some six intense months in an important event in the unfolding tragedy of the Province?

The immediate background lies in the escalating violence, civil disturbances and political turmoil in Northern Ireland in the late nineteen-sixties; the more remote one in the unusual and inflammatory socio-political and religious mix of the citizenry of Northern Ireland which encapsulated much of the inheritance of a bitter history. For those informed on these enduring matters no further explanation is necessary: for those not so endowed no explanation is possible. I need therefore spend no further time upon them, but I shall describe the immediate background in some more detail.

Following serious civil disturbance in Londonderry in early October 1968, further sporadic outbreaks occurred more widely despite various promised reform measures announced by the (Unionist) Prime Minister of Northern Ireland, Terence O'Neill, on 22nd November. These incidents reached a crescendo early in January when a march organised by a student's group, the People's Democracy, and the Civil Rights Association, which left Belfast for Londonderry on the 1st, and now enhanced with even more left-leaning groups, it was met en route mostly by threats and intimidation but also by actual serious violence notably at Burntollet Bridge and Irish Street on the outskirts of Londonderry. Terence O'Neill's Unionist government, now under pressure from the streets and with strong encouragement from Westminster, announced on 15th January that a wide-ranging Commission of Inquiry would be established; and on 3rd March, Lord Grey, the Governor of Northern Ireland, was able to announce the appointment of such a Commission with the terms of reference:

> to hold an enquiry into and to report upon the course of events leading to, and the immediate causes and nature of the violence and civil disturbance in Northern Ireland on and since 5th October 1968; and to assess the composition, conduct and aim of those bodies involved in the current agitation and in any incident arising out of it.

At the same time he was able to announce that he had appointed the Honourable Lord Cameron, D.S.C. as Chairman and with Professor Sir John Biggart, C.B.E. and James Joseph Campbell, Esq., M.A. as the other members. Lord Cameron was a distinguished High Court judge from Scotland, but his two colleagues may at first sight seem an unusual choice for a Commission with the stated terms of reference. However, they were selected after careful thought and extensive soundings. Identikits were first constructed. They should both be Ulstermen who could bring local knowledge to bear on the interpretation of events. They should be from either side of the politico-religious 'great divide' in Northern Ireland society. They should be widely known to be fair-minded persons of proven integrity and intellectual honesty. Neither should have had any active participation in politics nor any attachments to any political party. Neither should have an occupation or profession which might suggest an innate partiality in considering the evidence before the Commission. Clearly, in searching for such paragons and in the circumstances of Northern Ireland, the field of higher and further education should prove fruitful. Queen's was among those discreetly sounded. At the Cabinet meeting on 19th February 1969 the Cabinet Secretary, H. Black, put forward three names for consideration. To represent the Catholic-Nationalist 'side' the nominations were either (i) Mr J.J. Campbell, a highly respected member of the Queen's University Senate, a lecturer at St Joseph's College of Education and due to assume the Directorship of the Institute of Education at Queen's, or (ii) Professor James Scott, Professor of Dental Anatomy, a distinguished and popular academic but who had also well-known republican leanings. To represent the Unionist-Protestant community there was only one nomination, that of Sir John Biggart, Dean of the Medical Faculty and described by the Cabinet Secretary as 'perhaps the most distinguished academic at Queen's at the current time'. The Cabinet chose John Henry and J.J. Campbell: Professor Scott was eliminated on the basis that he was too closely identified with republicanism and also that his appointment, in tandem with my father, would have given a medico-dental slant, unjustifiable and certainly questionable in the circumstances. On the 28th February my father was startled to receive an official letter from the Prime Minister, Terence O'Neill – 'I know that you are a very busy man but if you could see your way to join the Commission, I and my colleagues would very much appreciate it'. Perhaps flattered to be chosen and never a man to evade a challenge, my father accepted. I think he felt that it was his opportunity to contribute in helping to find some solutions toward the 'Northern Ireland problem', especially curing the strife that had beset his beloved homeland since its inception. The Official Warrant of Appointment for Lord Cameron and his two fellow Commissioners to hold an enquiry with its terms of reference was granted by the Governor of Northern Ireland, Lord Grey of Naunton on 3rd March 1969.

A call for the public to submit evidence appeared in the press on 14th March 1969 and in addition a number of personal invitations were issued. The Commission soon got down to work and its procedures and findings are detailed in its Report published in September that year. Briefly, over the late spring and summer it considered submissions from 225 persons or bodies, representative of almost the entire spectrum of political and public opinions, and conducted many site visits and interviews. In all it met 26 times. Only five of those requested to give evidence declined: these included Mr William Craig MP and the Reverend Ian Paisley.

For more than 30 years the records of the evidence presented to the Commission was withheld by the Government, but the introduction of the Freedom of Information Act has of recent years made most of them available for public perusal. Only those that are deemed to endanger persons still alive are retained under wraps.

Inspection of these papers reveals the depths to which Lord Cameron and his two fellow-commissioners went to reach the truth behind the events. They probed the police and representatives from the Office of Home Affairs. They visited the areas of the disturbances and watched TV recordings. They took evidence from political parties, evidence from churches, evidence from various sections of the Civil Rights Movement and evidence from invited individuals from the public, including journalists. In these interviews it can be seen clearly how the local knowledge of J.J. Campbell and John Henry was particularly valuable in putting subtle pressure on politicians, the police and the marchers to justify their attitudes and actions.

Their intensive deliberations bore fruit with the publication of the Cameron Report in September 1969.* It was generally well received by the world press, particularly in the USA and in the Irish Republic. It had exposed unfairness in the delivery of Unionist rule towards the minority Catholic community, whilst finding the behaviour of the violent hangers-on on both sides totally irresponsible and unjustifiable. It tried to suggest a future way forward to correct injustices and to begin to heal the bitterness between the two communities. The threat of immediate civil war seemed to have been defused. However, the British press retained a significant degree of scepticism, as seen in the accompanying cartoon. From long years of experience they suspected that the Irish would never be at peace, they would only be content when looking for a brawl.* Unfortunately, their cynicism proved justified, the IRA was already laying sinister plans for the civil disruption that was to lead to a further 25 years of 'bomb and bullet'.

---

* *Disturbances in Northern Ireland*. Report of the Commission appointed by the Governor of Northern Ireland, September 1969. Belfast, Her Majesty's Stationery Office.
** *Daily Mail*, 13th September 1969.

'TIS ORLROIGHT MICK— THEY'RE ONLY DISCUSSIN' THE CAMERON REPORT!'

Daily Mail cartoon appearing immediately after the publication
of the Cameron Report, September 1969

The success of reports like that of the Cameron Commission can rarely
be judged in the aftermath of publication; only with the benefit of historical
assessment can a more accurate picture be reached. It is therefore of interest
that the late Arthur Green, a civil servant who was Secretary to the
Commission, originally fully supported the findings, but in an article in the
*Belfast Telegraph** 30 years later he had revised this opinion and expressed
the view that the Report was 'hasty, naïve and partisan in its criticism of
Unionism'. He now tended to sympathise with 'the predicament of the
Stormont Unionists, forced to govern where there could not be political
consensus, and caught between London's indifference and Dublin's malice'.

John Henry was pleased to have played his 'wee' part in trying to stem and
alleviate the deep rooted wounds of his 'wee Ulster'; but he lived for a further
decade, witnessing his countrymen at each others' throats. This caused him
great sadness. His political interlude was over. He had sampled its
frustrations and futility and was glad to return to his chosen world of
profession and family.

* Arthur Green in *Belfast Telegraph*, 13th September, 1999, p. 13.

159

Chapter 15

Twilight and after

On 31st July 1971 John Henry's unprecedented 27 years as the annually elected Dean of the Faculty of Medicine came to an end, and on 30th September so also did his unprecedented 34 year tenure of the Musgrave Chair of Pathology and his 23 years as the foundation Director of the Institute of Pathology. The preceding months had been marked by more than their customary bustle as valedictory functions hosted by each of the many organisations to which he had contributed so much over the years, mostly from a dominant position, were added to his normal activities. These latter were if anything more onerous than usual since they now included the pressing ones to do with the medical school in the light of the momentous national changes in the curriculum, student enrolment, continuing medical education (CME) and registration requirements, the radical restructuring of the General Medical Council, and the ever-present need for enabling finance, and all in the context of considerable social and political unrest as the most recent in the line of 'Troubles' entered their darkest phase.

Despite casual appearances my father's health was no longer robust: his hypertension and late onset, Type 2, insulin-treated diabetes, were at last taking their toll though he tried hard not to show it. Often, however, family and close friends noticed that his lips were cyanotic and that he panted on exertion most noticeably on climbing stairs. He was soon to develop angina at rest: at home I often noticed the knuckles of his left hand whiten from pressure as he dug his nails hard into his palm to avoid showing any signs of pain which would worry my mother sitting in the next chair. A few months before he retired, he actually collapsed one weekend semiconscious in his chair. He quickly partially recovered and I told him I was going to call a doctor. He grunted that 'he did not want any bloody doctor' though when I continued to press him he agreed to see Frank Pantridge. I got through to Frank at his home in Hillsborough and remarkably he arrived within 30 minutes and assumed complete control. Frank was now the doctor and John Henry was now his patient. Any residual resentment between them evaporated: 'Right John Henry, you have developed ventricular fibrillation. You are going to be alright and you are coming into my ward straightaway. You will soon be fine', and Frank, there and then drove him to the Royal where he was immediately defibrillated successfully. He returned home a few days later, extremely grateful that he was perhaps spared to live for a few more years.

The family naturally were concerned as to how his health would stand up to the many valedictory occasions (the principal ones were dinners given by the University, the Eastern Health and Social Services Board, the Royal Victoria Hospital and the Faculty of Medicine – who also commissioned his portrait – and the Institute of Pathology; but there were many others) with their eulogies for his achievements, the re-awakening of memories, the litanies of his many successes, and his mandatory speeches in reply; but though on occasions his voice wavered he disguised his deepest emotions and any signs of waning health, and his collection of fine china artefacts grew and grew as his interest as a collector became more widely known.

And now it was over: the man who had dominated so many aspects of Northern Ireland medicine was like any retiree, free to graze at leisure. But of course it wasn't all over, not by the longest shot; nor did he wish to graze, after all he still had many irons in the fire, notably membership of the General Medical Council and of the Northern Ireland Council for Postgraduate Medical and Dental Education of which he was Chairman-elect, and he was Chairman of the grandiloquently named Standing Medical Advisory Committee of the Ministry of Health, Northern Ireland, as well as giving freely of his time to many charitable bodies (listed in Appendix 3) and much more besides. Foremost in his mind as always, however, were the challenges to be faced by the Faculty of Medicine which would likely welcome (or at least need) his guidance, experience and advice and, where possible, relevant action, of which more below.

But, like many, he found it difficult to adjust to this new life but, unlike many, he didn't try very hard to do so! He continued to turn up frequently at the Institute of Pathology, stay for a time (not always short) spent mostly with the Acting Head, his close associate, Professor Florence McKeown, chat to the staff (they were all in his view of things *his* staff and in *his* Institute), and would often overstay his welcome and impede the flow of departmental

161

work. (When his successor in the Musgrave Chair, Dugald Gardner, arrived at the Institute on his first morning and tried to hang up his hat and coat in the professor's office, which was now his office, he found that John Henry had beaten him to the hat-stand).

Unquestionably the issues now before the Faculty were challenging and involved the introduction of the new undergraduate curriculum recommendations of the Todd Report, the development of multi-site clinical teaching facilities and more so-called 'academic clinical units' to accommodate also the requirements of 'Continuing Medical Education' (CME).*

Crucial to these would be the visitation by the Medical Sub-Committee of the University Grants Committee scheduled for 9th and 10th November that year, and to be lead by the formidable medical duo of Sir Robert Aitken and Sir Charles Stuart-Harris, respectively as Chairman and Vice-Chairman.

John Henry and the Dean-elect (Professor Peter Froggatt) had prepared an impressive, if optimistically acquisitive, Submission Paper for the occasion. Though he was no longer Dean nor even on the University staff, all hoped that John Henry could be in prominent and voluble attendance, as indeed he was. In the event Peter Froggatt, as the new Dean, led the Faculty 'team', who naturally argued forcefully in favour of the recommendations in their Submission and backed by my father in his most persuasive networking mode, as he led the members on strategically selected site visits (which included the eponymous Biggart House recently fully opened accommodation for clinical students beside the Royal Victoria Hospital), as well as indicating sweeping plans for the future frustrated only by lack of resources. These were to such good effect that Sir Robert, Sir Charles and their colleagues advised the main UGC that Queen's medical school should receive even more in 1973–8, by way of both capital and recurrent grants, than the Faculty had optimistically sought.

The details are in the records of the University, the Northern Ireland Hospitals Authority, the UGC and other involved bodies: but just to give a flavour, the UGC recommended 30,000 sq. ft (as against the 25,000 sq. ft sought) for clinical extension to the new Whitla Building beside the Belfast City Hospital, and 38,000 sq. ft for additional clinical teaching accommodation, not specifically sought, to be 'embedded' in the Hospital

* The Report of the Royal Commission on Medical Education, 1965–68, Cmnd 1968.

My mother unveiling photographic portrait of John Henry
at the opening of Sir John Biggart House (1971)

itself. ('Embedded' in UGC –speak meant 'under the same roof as' and not
just 'in an adjacent building to', which was then considered essential for the
success of a clinical academic unit). Since the hospital was being completely
rebuilt this necessitated altering the builders' contract at considerable
expense, none of which fell to the University to meet, and at considerable
embarrassment for some senior civil servants in Belfast who had to appear
before the Public Accounts Committee to explain the delay and additional

expense to the hospital re-building to include an extra 'teaching floor'. Also, a whopping 30% of the new recurrent monies over this period were to be reserved for the Faculty of Medicine. John Henry's wildest dreams, more accurately his firm convictions about *his* medical school, seemed about to be realised.

There were, however, several jokers in the pack – the 'Troubles', a possible fall from favour of the concept of 'embedded' multi-site clinical academic units, the collapse of the (favourable) settlement due to the then looming national financial crisis (something like this in fact happened from 1976) a lack of will on the part of the University to resist pleas from the other faculties who considered themselves relatively beggared by the largesse shown to Medicine, and various 'unknown unknowns'. John Henry knew he could do nothing about some of these, but he could about others providing he would still be an influence where it would count: nationally that meant continuing on the GMC; locally it meant becoming a prominent member of the Queen's governing body, the Senate (to frustrate any dilution of the UGC's settlement for Medicine), and a member of the new Postgraduate Medical and Dental Education Council – of which, not by chance, he was already chairman-elect!

Membership of the Senate would certainly be possible in one of the several categories of representative member, but continued membership of the GMC would be more difficult since, as from the moment of his retirement on 30th September 1971, he was no longer a member of the University (other than of Convocation as are all graduates), the very institution which he represented on the GMC. Peter Froggatt, however, persuaded the Vice-Chancellor, the ultra-scrupulous Sir Arthur Vick, that John Henry could and should continue at this crucial time; moreover, Froggatt stressed, the Presidency of the GMC would shortly be vacant on the retirement of Lord Cohen, and my father, as a long-standing and respected member and with Lord Cohen's encouragement (Cohen thought very highly of him and had been delighted when on my father's recommendation, he was invited by the Trustees to deliver the prestigious Wiles Lectures on the History of Civilisation, at Queen's in 1970) had hoped to stand and if successful would have been the first Irishman so honoured. No-one could reasonably deny him this unique opportunity, and although in the event Sir John (later Lord) Richardson, Bt, whose medical, social and 'establishment' credentials were admittedly impressive, was elected, within the year my father was appointed a Pro-Chancellor of Queen's which gave him the hoped-for senior Senate position and, importantly, it regularised his continued status as GMC 'representative member from Queen's', and he remained such until his death on 21st May 1979 only three months after he had relinquished the Chairmanship of the Postgraduate Medical Education Council. His broad imperium lasted little weakened until his death, though his exercise of power and influence was increasingly that of the *éminence grise* rather than of the benevolent despot which it had been for so long.

Dean Acheson, the American statesman, famously said of post-World War II Britain, that 'it has lost an Empire but hasn't yet found a role'. This might have been apt for Britain but it would never have fitted John Henry. On retirement my father certainly lost some of his Empire, notably the Chair of Pathology and the Deanship of the Faculty of Medicine, but he gained other territories, as mentioned above; while as for 'not yet finding a role', he didn't need to because he had never lost his, and he continued to play it clearly, unambiguously and with subtlety if with declining *brio* until the end.

On 21st May 1979, he flew to London to attend a meeting of the GMC. Professor Gerry Nelson and his wife Hazel travelled on the same plane to Heathrow and later commented that he was in his usual good form although complaining of not being able to walk any distance with comfort, presumably due to angina. As he entered the foyer of his hotel, Brown's Hotel in Dover Street, Piccadilly, he suddenly collapsed and died immediately. It was the way he had always hoped that he would go and it was befitting that his final journey was on behalf of the University that he so loved. Both his parents had died suddenly. He dreaded the thought of a more lingering illness, such as a stroke. He knew that his temperament would have borne such incapacity with total frustration. A coroner's post-mortem examination revealed that he had succumbed to a massive heart attack. My mother, sister and I were shattered at our sudden loss. Some days after the cremation at Roselawn Cemetery I was going through his belongings which had been returned by the hotel. On opening his diary, a little newspaper-cutting fluttered to the floor. It was a quotation, which read 'the things, which I have seen, I now can see no more' (from 'The Intimations of Immortality' by William Wordsworth).

Amongst the innumerable letters of sympathy was one from H.C. Fay, the brilliant though eccentric Head Teacher of the Classical Department at Inst. I can almost hear his strident tones as he included in his letter: 'My knowledge of him was as an admirable parent, who saw to it that his son, destined to his own medical profession, should learn some Latin and Greek.' He ended: ' "Magnus civis obit" ... Biggart, boy, translate!'

Always the obedient pupil, I shall now comply:

'The Great Citizen is Dead'

John Henry in his Queen's University Pro-Chancellor gown (1971)

APPENDIX 1

Degrees and honours

C.B.E. 1948

K.B.E. 1968

M.B. (Hons.) 1928

M.D. (Gold Medal) 1931

Commonwealth Fellowship to Johns Hopkins, Baltimore 1931–3

D.Sc. 1937

Robert Campbell Orator, Ulster Medical Society 1948

M.R.C.P. 1952

F.R.C.P. 1957

Hon. M.D. Trinity College, Dublin 1957

Honorary Fellowship of Irish Medical Laboratory Technicians
(Belfast branch) 1963

F.R.C. Path. 1964

Hon. Member of James IV Association of Surgeons 1964

Hon. F.R.C.P.I. 1969

Hon. F.R.G.P. 1971

Hon. L.L.D. Queen's University, Belfast 1971

Hon. D.Sc. National University of Ireland 1973

Hon. Fellow of Ulster Medical Society 1977

APPENDIX 2

Career posts

Pathologist to Scottish Asylums' Board 1933–7

Lecturer in Neuropathology, Edinburgh University 1933–7

Professor of Pathology, Queen's University, Belfast 1937–71

Director of Institute of Pathology, Queen's University, Belfast 1948–71

Dean of the Faculty of Medicine, Queen's University, Belfast 1944–71

Regional Director of Blood Transfusion Service 193[9]–46

Member of Queen's University Senate 1948–71

Pro-Vice-Chancellor, Queen's University, Belfast 1967–71

Pro-Chancellor, Queen's University, Belfast 1972–9

Committees

Chairman, Laboratory Services Committee, Northern Ireland Hospitals Authority (NIHA) 1948–54

Chairman, Medical Education and Research Committee, NIHA 1950–64

Member of General Medical Council, London 1951–79

Member of General Dental Council, London 1959–79

Member of General Medical Council (Irish branch) 1971–9

Chairman of Standing Medical Advisory Committee, Ministry of Health, N.I. 1967–73

Member of Council, College of Pathologists 1968

Chairman, Northern Ireland Council of Postgraduate Medical Education 1971–9

Member of Central Medical Advisory Committee, Ministry of Health, N.I. 1974–6

APPENDIX 3

Involvement in charitable organisations

British Empire Cancer Campaign
Belfast Home for the Blind
Marie Curie Beaconsfield Home for Cancer Care
Northern Ireland Mental Association
Northern Ireland Multiple Sclerosis Society
Northern Ireland Muscular Dystrophy Association
Ulster Cancer Foundation
Age Concern

APPENDIX 4

**The poetry and verse of
John Henry Biggart**

ATOMIC DEATH

The quiet of the molecule
Throbs with the passion of dismemberment
And angry hordes of anarchy
Sting matter to activity.
Neutrons, electrons, gamma, beta rays
Mushroom towards the sky.
The earth is seared,
And in one blinding flash
The stored up energy of aeons
Flings itself free.

After the devastation of noise
The still small voice
Calls the last human souls.
Immaterial, unionisable
Majestically they sail
Through ways impassable to matter
Back to their God.

Whilst on the earth
The dust rains down
The final pall
Upon the global cemetery.

BELFAST 1972

A public house has gone,
The social club of weary working men
And on the pavement lie the blood stained bodies
And screaming women gather round
And tear stained faces clasp to themselves
Their maimed partners.

Then from forth the flames, brave men
Bring forth the stretcher, with body shrouded,
And women lose their fears and stand white faced
Dry eyed, but tense
Before their temporary bier.

Why did it happen?
What did they do it for?
What matter was the colour of a flag?
It was humanity that suffered
From the unthinking folly of unthinking thugs.

No cause,
No flag
Is worth the sacrifice of human life,
Yet now from out the silence comes the sound of bomb and bullet
And all the hellish death begins again.

So might one well despair,
Yet somehow as the dawn succeeds the night
There is the rational hope
That man will soldier on and peace will come.

The wailing of the women may prevail
Or common sense or the vast inertia of those who still see life
As worthy to be lived unrecompensed.

How marvellous it would be
If pape could live with prod,
And somehow recreate life's majesty.

CHRISTMAS NIGHT 1973

Old men should fight
Not sit complacently
And pass from lightness into dark.
The young will have their way
With loins untired
They drive unwittingly
To the next day's dawn.
The wisdom of the centuries
They scorn
And knowing everything
They seek the morn.
Yet seeking,
They will tread
The self-same paths
And turn to wise old sages
Who failed, as they will fail.
Yet did they fail
Those old wise sages?
Something or things
They kept alive.
The feeling of newness
In each dawn
The feeling that man was more
Than chemists could explain.
The hope that mankind could live
If man could expiate his hate
That knowledge was not everything
That beauty, love could mate.
So old men fight
Hard to his aggressive youth
The wisdom of the ages
The mellowness that comes with years
The panacea for rebellious tears.

WAY BACK FROM THE ROAD

Let me live for a time way back from the road
Where very few folks go by
With some books, a few friends, and a woodland trail
And above me a clear blue sky
I'm willing to work all the days of the week
And most of the hours each day
But I do want a house way back from the road
Where I sometimes can get away.

Let me see from my house way back from the road
Bright flowers and a bird that sings
Where no one can tell me of grief and pain
And a telephone never rings
I would turn not away from the sorrows and aches
That seem to be part of my life
If at times I could get away back from the road
And escape for a time the strife.

There are times when I must get me back from the road
And permit mankind to go by:
It suffers, it sorrows:
With its grief, with its pain –
Shared in it all have I.
I seem a part of the grief of the world
With myriads of men.
So at times I must rest me way back from the road
Then share it all over again.

MY LITTLE BROWN BAT

I smoked my pipe
I drank my nightcap
I read my book
I went to bed.
The light I turned out
Then from the darkness
Came a miniscule squeak
Repeated interminably.
A pair of beating wings
Zoomed on my forehead,
Feathered my nose
And almost kissed my lips.
Still in the darkness of the night
Came miniscule squeak and squeak
Whilst furry wings
Fanned one's excited face.
I turned my light on
And I saw
Fluttering against the curtains
A little brown bat.
I seized my Paisley dressing gown

And as a matador
Before his bull
Stood ready to attack
Wave after wave I made
But always the little bat
At the last moment
Eluded all my effort
But finally in a vast
Umbrella wave
Which swept the ceiling
My gown enwrapt the bat
Beneath my snatching hands
I feel the small body
Pulsating with a heart beat
That betrayed its terror
So gently did I bear it
To the window
And gently shake my gown
And out into the night
Went the winged miniscule squeak
My little brown bat.

AUTUMN

The evenings darken, night comes soon,
Again one reads by lamplight not by sun,
And autumn mistiness does mask the morn.

And in the garden everything shows change
The wild rose fades, each flower replaced
By rounded hip that gleams
In the faint light of the departing sun.

The branches of the apple tree
Are bent with swelling fruit
Whose colour changes first to gold
Then lights with crimson glow.

But the sweet autumnal sun
Furnishes some flowers with life,
The roses still do bloom
Amid their petals bees still hum.

Sweet scents still fill the evening air,
The swallows gather on the wire,
Still in the morning comes bird song
For winter is not yet, it's still to come.

ENVOI*

In a full medical life
I have sought to understand
Why people die
Not the simple things
Like bodies crushed
In accidents
Or dying suddenly
With bullets in their brains
Or choked with chemical dust
Or drowned.
Rather to find
Why ordinary people die
Their bodies worn out
And suddenly become incompetent.
So have I travailed
Over the years
And sought the answer
Each death
A problem to be solved
Hoping each problem understood
Would bring some knowledge
To prevent the same thing
Happening again.
With expertise I carved
Each sterno-clavicular joint
With care
Cracked each and every rib
Exposed the thorax
Fondled every heart.
Transected every lung

* Biggart, J.H.: 'Envoi': *Ulster Medical Journal*, 1983; vol. 52(1): pp 75–6.

Sought out the thymus
Examined every lymph-node
Drew down the larynx
Tonsils and glottis
Weighed the thyroid
Found the parathyroids,
With care
I sectioned the abdomen
Carved gently the liver
And sought to find
If bile ducts were intact
Or whether some abstruse condition
Had altered
The content of the tissue.
Each kidney split in half
Cortex and medulla compared
The volume of the pelvises
The patency of the ureters
All were sought
To further diagnosis.
Adrenals, testes, ovaries,
Pancreas, all contributed
Their tiny quota
Of evidence.
The brain
Wherein we thought
The final evidence
Would be found
Was specially prepared
But though we sought
We found but little

To explain
Final catastrophe.
In Mrs X.
We seemed to find
An answer
To our quandary.
But Mrs Y.
Had much more wrong
Yet somehow managed
To survive
Her heart was worn
Her kidneys far from normal
Her head had no cause
To function
Her brain was small
No larger than her rival
And yet she lived
More joyfully and longer
Until she died
Beneath a bus.
And so I wonder
If our facile explanations
Are quite as valid
As we seem
To make them
And whether
Individuals
Have not some say
In how
Their various diseases
Affect them.

DESIRES

Give me the joyous life I love
And I'll not ask for more:
A night to revel, a day to rove
And peace when all is o'er.

Give me a book that I can read
A book of love and life
Wherein I'll read of many a deed
Of friendship and of strife.

Give me a girl that I can love
As I, oh my love, love thee.
Then can I scale the heavens above
And triumph on land and sea.

For few are the things that I desire
But those few I love well
And through my life I'll never tire
In stirring sounds to tell
Of the night I revelled, the day I roved,
The book I read, and the girl I loved

VENEZ! AIMONS NOUS

Venez! Aimons nous
Déjà la nuit descend
Déjà la lune monte
Alors dépêchez vous.

Venez! Aimons nous
Commençons-nous a vivre
Et a amir. Venez!
Pourquoi restez-vous?

La lune est montée
Les étoiles étincellent.
C'est le temps pour l'amour
C'est le temps d'aimer.

La lune pâlit
Les étoiles se cachent
La nuit s'évanouit
Jamais l'amour ne finit.

Tout va passer déjà:
La mort engloutit tout;
Mais l'amour durera
Tant que l'homme vivra.

Tout a le dessous
Dans la vie, hors d'amour.
Qui existe malgré' tout
Alors! Aimons-nous!

LOVE IN ABSENCE

Remember me when I am gone away
Gone far away unto another place
Where I no more can look into your face
Smiling in welcome, entreating you to stay.
Remember me when I can no longer say
Sweet words of joy and love to you or trace
The marks of ever-present care upon your face,
Or reason how to smooth them all away.
Fair days will come, delay awhile, and go.
Dark nights will follow, urging us to sleep.
With night sweet visions come, our thoughts will flow
Back to each other, quickening us to keep
Remembrance of our love, which thus will grow
And spring up in our hearts, more strong, more deep.

TO ADMIRANDA

It's golden like the setting sun
My darling's eyes are bright and blue
Her lips are cherry red
And the snowdrop with its crown of white
Envies her pale forehead.
And when she smiles the dimples play
Upon her pretty cheeks
And her little mouth now tempts, entices –
Now blushes fire her cheeks.
And her hair hangs most bewitchingly
In clusters round her head
When the lightsome day is sped.

EVENING

Fast falls the shimmering twilight on the plain
The blood-red sun descends behind the hill
Some thrush still twitters in yon winding lane
But soon his song is o'er and all is still.
The honeysuckled flowers distill their perfumed dew
Which incense-breathing hangs amid the trees;
Or gently wafted on to thickets new
Exhales its perfume to the wand'ring breeze.
The ghostly trees sway gently to and fro
As if in anger 'gainst the wakeful winds
Once more the silence falls, solemn, slow,
Its silent guards, the tall and slender pines.
A tearful band of children homewards run
Dreading their mother's wrath and anxious tears
But dreading more, the darkness and the sinking sun.
Onwards they hasten with increasing fears.
The gathering darkness deepens and black night
Descends in triumph, stealing from the north
It takes the land within its grip of might
And shrouds its beauty, till the moon shines forth.
Darkening I listen, and for many a time
 I have been half in love with easeful death.
Sing on, sweet bird, comfort life-weary man.
 Pour forth thy melodies increasingly
 Till thou hast filled the world with sounds so sweet
 As those which raised the sleeping Caliban.
Thy song now mounts up higher, loud and full,
 Now soft and low it calms impassioned hearts
 Still lower, the weary sink in rest
 And in the land of dreams, in peace they rule.
Sing on, sweet bird, in that melodious strain.
 So could I listen whilst the years glide past
 Lulled by thy song and the sweet smelling breeze
 Care-free and happy in the peaceful lane.
Alas! These thoughts are over! Thy song is o'er.
Thee I shall hear no more, no never more.

APPENDIX 5

Publications

Biggart J.H., *Pathology of the Nervous System*. 1st edition 1936, reprinted 1940, 2nd edition 1949, 3rd edition 1961. E.S. Livingstone, Edinburgh.

* * * * * * * * * * *

Biggart J.H., Drennan A.M., 'Eosinophile leukaemia', *Journal of Laboratory and Clinical Medicine* 1924; 9: 803.

Biggart J.H., Drennan A.M., 'Persistent eosinophilia', *Journal of Pathology and Bacteriology* 1930; 33: 995–1002.

Biggart, J.H., Stewart H.H., 'A case of acute bronchiolectasis', *British Medical Journal* 1931; 1: 1115.

Biggart J.H., 'Some observations on the eosinophile cell' *Journal of Pathology and Bacteriology* 1932; 35: 799–816.

Biggart J.H., 'The Role of the Anterior Hypophysis in the Child', *Ulster Medical Journal* 1933; 2(4): 288–92.

Biggart J.H., 'The origin of the eosinophil granule', *Ulster Medical Journal* 1933; 2: 47–52.

Biggart J.H., 'Actinomycosis graminis', *Bulletin of Johns Hopkins Hospital*, 1934; 54:165.

Biggart J.H., 'The hypophysis of the human castrate', *Bulletin of Johns Hopkins Hospital* 1934; 54: 157.

Biggart J.H., 'Diabetes Insipidus', *Brain* 1935; 58(1): 86–96.

Biggart J.H., 'Some observations on the basophil cells of the human hypophysis', *Edinburgh Medical Journal* 1935; 42: 113–24.

Biggart J.H., 'Diabetes insipidus', *Edinburgh Medical Journal* 1936; 43: 417.

Biggart J.H., Dott N.M., 'Pituitary tumours, their classification and treatment', *British Medical Journal* 1936; 2: 1153–5.

Biggart J.H., Dott N.M., 'Pituitary tumours and their classification and treatment' *British Medical Journal*; 1936; 2: 1206–08.

Biggart J.H., Page A.P.M., Roberts L.V., 'Cushing's syndrome in a mulatto', *Lancet* 1937; 2: 625–7.

Biggart J.H., 'Human infection with fasciola hepatica', *Journal of Pathology* 1937; 44: 488–9.

Biggart J.H., 'The anatomical basis for resistance to pituitrin in diabetes insipidus', *Journal of Pathology and Bacteriology* 1937; 44: 305–14.

Biggart J.H., 'Diabetes Insipidus, The Role of the Anterior Hypophysis'. *Ulster Medical Journal* 1938; 7(2): 115–19.

Biggart J.H., Fisher J.A. 'Meningo-encephalitis complicating Herpes Zoster', *Lancet* 1938; 232: 944–6.

Biggart J.H., Alexander G.L., 'Experimental Diabetes insipidus', *The Journal of Pathology and Bacteriology* 1939; 48(2): 405–25.

Biggart J.H., Campbell A.C.P., 'Wernicke's encephalopathy (polioencephalitis haemorraghica superior) its alcoholic and non-alcoholic incidence', *Journal of Pathology* 1939; 48: 245–62.

Biggart J.H., Campbell A.C.P., 'Pesticidal diabetes', *Journal of Pathology and Bacteriology* 1939; 48: 245.

Biggart J.H., 'Generalised Neurofibromatosis', *Ulster Medical Journal* 1941; 10(2): 77–82, 83–7.

Biggart J.H., 'Simmonds' Disease', *Ulster Medical Journal* 1941; 10(2) 87–90, 91–3.

Biggart J.H., Allen F.M.B., Macafee C.M.G., 'Neonatal mortality', *British Journal of Obstetricians and Gynaecologists* 1943; 50: 417–26.

Biggart J.H., 'Acute Monocytic Leukaemia', *Ulster Medical Journal* 1945; 14(1): 10–16.

Biggart J.H., 'The Contribution of Pathology to our Knowledge of the Internal Environment', *Ulster Medical Journal* 1948; 17(1): 1–14, 15–19.

Biggart J.H., 'Parergon', *Ulster Medical Journal* 1949; 18(2): 116–18, 119–28.

Biggart J.H., 'Isolated (Fiedler's) Myocarditis', *Ulster Medical Journal* 1950; 19(1): 59–66.

Biggart J.H., Macafee C.H.G., 'Tumours of the Ovarian mesenchyme and their gonadal relationships', *American Journal of Gynecology* 1955; 86: 1021–6

Biggart J.H., Macafee C.H.G., 'Tumours of the ovarian mesenchyme', *British Journal of Obstetrics and Gynaecology* 1955; 62(6): 829–37.

Biggart J.H., Willis J., 'Peptic ulceration and endocrine disease in necropsy material', *Lancet* 1959; 274: 938–9.

Biggart J.H., 'Medical Education-Editorial', *Ulster Medical Journal* 1962; 31(2): 142–3.

Biggart J.H., 'The Future of Medical Education-Editorial', *Ulster Medical Journal* 1963; 32(2): 139–40.

Biggart J.H., 'The future of disease', *Physiotherapy* 1964; 50: 355–9.

Biggart J.H., 'Address at Special Graduation ceremony in Queen's University for the British Dental Association meeting on 23rd June 1965', *Ulster Medical Journal* 1965; 34(1): 8–10.

Biggart J.H., 'Whither education? The challenge of nurse education', *Nursing Times* 1968; 64 (23): Suppl: 89–92.

Biggart J.H., 'The challenge of nurse education', *Internal Nursing Review* 1968; 15: 292–307.

Biggart J.H., 'Cnidos v Cos – Presidential Address to Ulster Medical Society', *Ulster Medical Journal* 1972; 41(1): 1–9.

Biggart J.H., Kernoghan R.J., 'Postgraduate Medical Education in Northern Ireland', *Ulster Medical Journal* 1974; 43(1): 71–3.

Biggart J.H., 'Envoi', *Ulster Medical Journal* 1983; 52(1): 75–6.

INDEX